I generally buy books according to author first, then the subject. Eddie and Alice have been my friends for more than three decades. I would choose their book on both bases. They have effectively combined fresh insights, touching illustrations, scriptural principles and a unique legal setting to present to us an elevated view of prayer.

—Dr. Jack Taylor
Dimensions in Christian Living

Eddie and Alice Smith take us into the world of the divine court to vividly remind us that "we have an advocate with the Father, Jesus Christ the righteous" (1 John 2:1, KJV). This biblically based and innovative approach broadens our understanding of the privilege and power of intercessory prayer.

—Doug Beacham, Superintendent
Georgia Conference
International Pentecostal Holiness Church

The Advocates by Eddie and Alice Smith provides the most powerful and persuasive picture of the true role of an intercessor that I have ever read. Every praying believer needs this message.

—Dr. Dick Eastman, International President
Every Home for Christ

The Advocates inspires new levels of maturity and victory in both personal and corporate prayer opportunities! It will dramatically impact your prayer experiences! Absorb the dynamic principles of *biblically presenting your case before the throne of grace,* and transformation is inevitable!

—Bane and Barbara James
World Intercession Network

At last, amazing insight into how God likes to be approached! *The Advocates* provides us with an easy-to-understand study of how God wants us to pursue our cases in HIS courtroom. An invaluable handbook for intercessors.

—Bill and Connie Fisher, Chairman
Board of Directors, U.S. PRAYER CENTER

D0170333

The Advocates

EDDIE & ALICE SMITH

Charisma®
HOUSE
Books about Spirit-Led Living

THE ADVOCATES by Eddie and Alice Smith
Published by Charisma House
A part of Strang Communications Company
600 Rinehart Road
Lake Mary, Florida 32746
www.charismahouse.com

Unless otherwise noted, all Scripture quotations are from the
Holy Bible, New International Version. Copyright © 1973,
1978, 1984, International Bible Society. Used by permission.

Scripture quotations marked KJV are from the King James
Version of the Bible.

Scripture quotations marked NRSV are from the New Revised
Standard Version of the Bible. Copyright © 1989 by the Division
of Christian Education of the National Council of the Churches
of Christ in the USA. Used by permission.

Scripture quotations marked RSV are from the Revised Standard
Version of the Bible. Copyright © 1946, 1952, 1971 by the
Division of Christian Education of the National Council of the
Churches of Christ in the USA. Used by permission.

Library of Congress Catalog Card Number: 00-111897
International Standard Book Number: 0-88419-756-5

01 02 03 04   7 6 5 4 3 2
Printed in the United States of America

To our children:
Robert, Julia, Bryan and Ashlee.
We love you!

Acknowledgments

We would like to thank these Christian attorneys who took time to explain some legal terms and procedures. We appreciate each of you.

Attorney Tony Aninao, Houston, TX
Attorney Roger Bridgwater, Houston, TX
Attorney Jim Brown, Houston, TX
Attorney Peter Costea, Houston, TX
Attorney George Meijlander, Houston, TX

Many thanks to our sixty-one personal intercessors and our Board of Directors, without whom we would have never made it this far!

Contents

Chapter 1

The Trials of Life

*An intercessor means one who is in such vital
contact with God and with his fellowmen that he is like
a live wire closing the gap between the saving power of God
and the sinful men who have been cut off from that power.*
—HANNAH HURNARD

INSIDE the spacious ivory courtroom, heaven's bailiff stands to his feet and walks toward the huge imposing doors leading to the Judge's private chambers.

"All rise," he announces sternly to those assembled.

We immediately stand to our feet. Everyone is breathless, and every eye is fixed on the massive doors.

Suddenly the doors swing open, and everyone gasps. The Judge of the Universe, the Honorable Judge Jehovah of the Eternal Court of heaven, steps from the portal of His private chamber in the majesty of His splendor. His long, white glistening robe twirls as He spins and seats Himself upon a royal throne.

"Be seated," His authoritative voice thunders. We drop to our seats in rapt attention.

Seated to the Judge's right and to our left is the defendant, Cheryl, a young wife and mother of three who is sickly and frail. Cheryl trembles. Anxiety is etched upon her pale face. Somehow we know that she is afraid of the unknown.

But who is the sinister-looking fellow who is moving toward her? Wait! That's Satan, the prosecutor, the accuser of the brethren. He's a bad character. He has only three things on his mind: to steal, to kill and to destroy Cheryl.

Now it's clear to us—Satan has leveled a charge against this loving wife and mother. The charge? It's a case of terminal cancer.

Judge Jehovah reads the charge quietly to Himself and moans sadly. Looking up He asks the assembly, "Who is this lady's attorney?"

There is no immediate answer, only silence.

"Would the counsel for the defense please make your presence known," the Judge urges. The eerie echo of death permeates the room, as no one utters a word.

The Judge emphatically asks, "Is there counsel here today who is ready to plead this woman's case?"

After a moment of awkward silence, the compassionate Judge looks lovingly into Cheryl's troubled eyes and tenderly asks, "Daughter, who is your defense attorney?"

Warm tears wash Cheryl's face. She bows and slowly turns her head from side to side, shrugging her shoulders helplessly. Who will defend her?

An advocate must defend her. But what is an advocate? In court, an *advocate* is an attorney who speaks on behalf of a client. Advocacy is similar to intercession. An *intercessor* is one who stands in the gap for others (as their advocate) in prayer. Beloved, if one of us is not interceding on Cheryl's—and the millions of others like her—behalf, they have no earthly defense attorney. They are without advocacy to protest the actions of the evil one. No one wants to go to trial without an attorney!

TRIALS ABOUND

Who will defend them in their hour of trial? Most Americans live in a self-centered "me, myself and I" culture. We are busy looking out for number one! Many of us try every other option before we turn to prayer. And when we do pray, it's to get our own needs met after we have exhausted every other source and resource and have no place else to turn. Prayer is often our *last resort*—not our *first response*. Prayerlessness has rendered the church powerless and virtually irrelevant in American society.

We must learn how to become spiritual intercessory advocates. We do so by defending the causes of others. Defending another is a stretch for some who spend their time judging and accusing others. By their actions, they are offering themselves as witnesses for the devil's prosecution. Let's help change this.

We know from personal experience how important it is to have those who will defend us in prayer during our trials. At one time we were on staff at a church that was unfamiliar with the ministry of deliverance. One day our senior pastor called to ask for an appointment with us. He said that it was important, but it would be better if he waited until after we arrived to explain exactly why he needed to see us.

The day we arrived for our mysterious appointment we casually walked in and settled into our chairs. Pastor Lane* walked in, shaking his head in disbelief. "You are not going to believe what I'm about to tell you!" he told us.

"What happened? Tell us what is bothering you." I (Alice) said.

"Eddie and Alice, Mrs. Jenkins** is telling our church members that you are a warlock and a witch!"

Eddie laughed aloud. "You're kidding, right?" Eddie smiled.

"This is no joke," Pastor Lane continued. "Alice, remember when you came back from youth camp and told me that several of the teens had gotten saved but needed deliverance? For the sake of not embarrassing them, you took them into another room for a deliverance prayer. Remember?"

"Yes, Pastor, that is exactly what we did. We also felt that taking them to another room provided the least amount of distraction for the rest of the group," I reconfirmed.

"Well, Alice, Mrs. Jenkins believes that you were taking the youth to another room to perform incantations in order to convert them to witchcraft," Pastor Lane replied in a puzzled tone of voice.

We asked for, and received, his permission to meet with our accuser, Mrs. Jenkins, the next morning.

That night in prayer, we asked the Lord what we should do. We felt the Lord told us not to speak in our own defense, but instead let our pastor guide the conversation. Slightly anxious, but confident of our strategy, we went to bed.

When we stepped into Pastor Lane's office the next day,

---

* Not his real name
** Not her real name

Mrs. Jenkins was waiting for us. We felt like lambs being led to the slaughter as we listened, yet said nothing. Not long into the conversation between her and Pastor Lane, she suddenly had a change of heart. She began repenting nervously, telling us that she didn't know why she passed this accusation around the church. She said that all along she knew it wasn't true.

We never spoke one word until after our pastor had resolved the entire issue. Relieved and grateful to the Lord, we thanked Mrs. Jenkins for the apology, prayed for her and blessed her.

Every Christian will face Satan's attacks from time to time. Some will be severe, others not so severe. We are all engaged in a great spiritual battle with the enemy. After all, this is war!

Trials abound, don't they? If you are not in a trial, it is probably because you have just emerged from one, or you are about to face one. Quite often, *we* ourselves are the defendants in need of an attorney. (See 1 Peter 4:12–16.)

But a great prayer revolution is occurring in our nation. In the midst of crumbling American morals, school and workplace shootings, pervasive sexual perversion and natural disasters, more and more Christians are engaging in intercessory prayer. They are beginning to understand and accept their roles as God's spiritual defense attorneys who (as advocates) plead for mercy on behalf of those the devil brings to trial.

PERSONAL TRIALS

Have you ever considered the similarity between life's trials, which we all must face, and a court trial? This book was written to reveal this comparison. There is much we can learn about intercessory prayer by looking at the methods attorneys employ in the courtroom.

For example: Why are we being tried? Peter teaches that the eternal reward we have in Christ is being "kept in heaven" for us.

Praise be to the God and Father of our Lord Jesus Christ! In his great mercy he has given us new birth into a living hope through the resurrection of Jesus Christ from the dead, and into an inheritance that can never perish, spoil or fade—kept in heaven for you, who through faith are shielded by God's power until the coming of the salvation that is ready to be revealed in the last time. In this you greatly rejoice, though now for a little while you may have had to suffer grief in all kinds of trials. These have come so that your faith—of greater worth than gold, which perishes even though refined by fire—may be proved genuine and may result in praise, glory and honor when Jesus Christ is revealed.

—1 Peter 1:3–7

Peter says that between now and the time we fully receive our reward, we will suffer trials. However, we shouldn't be surprised or discouraged. He explains that these trials come so that our faith may be refined and purified like precious gold.

Jewelers work with different purities of gold. There is gold-plated, gold-filled, 10K, 14K, 18K and 24K gold. Master designers will tell you that the purer the gold, the softer it is. The same is true in our lives—the trials of our lives, like a refiner's fire, burn away impurities. As a result, a softening takes place in our lives that makes us pliable and more easily conformed into the image of Christ. (See Romans 8:29.) Our lives then result in praise, glory and honor to Christ!

Yes, trials are part of God's plan for us!

In Acts 9 we read of pompous Saul of Tarsus who was threatening to kill Christians. This angry religious zealot, who would later become Paul the Apostle, had received permission from the high priest to travel to Damascus in search of Christians. His job was to arrest them and bring them back to stand trial in Jerusalem.

The Trials of Life

In the 1970s there was a Christian song titled "A Funny Thing Happened on the Way to Hell—I Got Saved, Saved, Saved!" Well, a funny thing happened to Saul on his way to Damascus. Allow us to paraphrase Paul's experience as recorded in Acts 9:3–16.

Suddenly a light from heaven flashed around Saul. His horse, surprised by the flash of lightning, bolted and threw Saul unceremoniously to the ground where he heard a voice say to him, "Saul, Saul, why are you persecuting Me?"

(Can't you almost visualize Saul, like Fred Sanford on the old television sitcom *Sanford and Son*, grabbing his chest and announcing, "This is the BIG one!") No doubt stunned by the question, Saul asked, "Who are you?"

"I am Jesus. Saul, it is Me whom you are really persecuting," Jesus replied. "Now get up off the ground and go into the city where I will give you further instructions."

The men traveling with Saul were dumbfounded. They heard the voice, but they saw nothing.

When Saul stood up, he was blind as a bat—totally blind! His friends led him by the hand, like a child, into Damascus where he stayed for three days, during which time he did not eat or drink anything.

A disciple named Ananias lived in Damascus. He would have almost certainly been one of the people Saul would have sought out, arrested and taken to Jerusalem to stand trial.

While Ananias was praying he heard the Lord call his name.

"Yes, Lord," he answered.

The Lord said, "Ananias, go to the house of Judas on Straight Street and ask to speak to Saul of Tarsus."

"Lord, there must be some mistake," Ananias nervously answered. "Bad news travels fast around here. Don't You know that he has been persecuting Christians in Jerusalem? It's been said that he has come here to arrest me, and anyone else who calls on Your name. This might not be a safe thing for me to do."

"I know all of that, Ananias," the Lord explained. "At this moment he's blind, helpless and praying to Me. In fact, I just showed him in a vision how you will come and place your hands on him to restore his sight. I have chosen this Saul of Tarsus as an instrument to carry My name before the Gentiles and their kings and before the people of Israel. I will show him how much he must suffer for My name."

Ananias was startled by His words: *Suffer?* he thought. *Did He say "suffer" for My name? Shouldn't the Christian life be trouble free? What kind of message is this to share with a new believer? I can hear it now, "Mr. Tarsus? Uh, may I call you Saul? My name is Ananias. I am delighted to report that God has chosen to honor you with the privilege of suffering for Christ." Great news, huh?*

Trials are a part of God's plan for us. When a strong-willed zealot like Saul begins steamrolling his way through life, God has ways of arranging circumstances to capture his attention. This was necessary for Saul. And suffer he did! Just look at what he says:

Are they servants of Christ? (I am out of my mind to talk like this.) I am more. I have worked much harder, been in prison more frequently, been flogged more severely, and been exposed to death again and again. Five times I received from the Jews the forty lashes minus one. Three times I was beaten with rods, once I was stoned, three times I was shipwrecked. I spent a night and a day in the open sea, I have been constantly on the move. I have been in danger from rivers, in danger from bandits, in danger from my own countrymen, in danger from Gentiles; in danger in the city, in danger in the country, in danger at sea; and in danger from false brothers. I have labored and toiled and have often gone without sleep; I have known hunger and thirst and have often gone without food; I have been cold and naked. Besides everything else, I face daily the pressure of my concern for all the churches.

—2 CORINTHIANS 11:23–28

God's plan was for Saul, later known as Paul the Apostle, to suffer so that he could identify with the struggles of the Gentiles, the poor, women, children and the sick. If God had not broken his controlling, domineering soul of its pharisaic legalism, he never could have been used as God's voice to the masses.

He was also allowed to suffer in order to break the hard outer shell of his soul so that the fragrant life of the Spirit could be released. Out of Paul's weakness, God's strength could finally be displayed.

WE ARE NOT THE FIRST

Yes, suffering *is* part of the plan. It's little comfort, we know. But, we are not the first to "stand trial." In 2 Corinthians 8:1–2, Paul described the results of the trial suffered by the Macedonian Christians. "And now, brothers, we want you to know about the grace that God has given the Macedonian churches. Out of the most severe trial, their overflowing joy and their extreme poverty welled up in rich generosity." The key to our victory comes when we understand God's ways of using our trials for His glory. At that point, we can express joy even in the middle of our difficulties.

Sometimes surprise blessings are hidden in unfortunate life experiences. Such was the case in a story told by Rev. H. C. Trumbull:

Rev. H. C. Trumbull told the story of a poor man whose small mill and home were washed away by a flood.

Everything he had in the world was gone, and as he stood on the site, heart-broken and discouraged, he saw something shining in the bank, which the waters had washed bare. It was gold. The flood, which had beggared him, made him rich.[1]

No doubt that man thanked God for the adverse circumstances that actually brought him wealth. We too shall thank God someday for what we thought were losses due to life's calamities. In reality, for most of us, the life experiences that have done the most to shape us into the image of Christ have not been things we would have placed on our "to do" list or our list of life goals. They were seldom things we would have naturally desired.

Hebrews 11 has been called "Faith's Hall of Fame." About these "Hall of Fame-ers," Hebrews 11:13–16 says this:

> All these people were still living by faith when they died. They did not receive the things promised; they only saw them and welcomed them from a distance. And they admitted that they were aliens and strangers on earth. People who say such things show that they are looking for a country of their own. If they had been thinking of the country they had left, they would have had opportunity to return. Instead, they were longing for a better country—a heavenly one. Therefore God is not ashamed to be called their God, for he has prepared a city for them.

These people didn't receive entrance to Faith's Hall of Fame by living comfortable, trouble-free lives. Their faith was birthed in adversity, grew through displacement and rejection and blossomed in unrealized hopes and dreams. Take a closer look at these heroes of the faith:

- Abraham was asked to offer Isaac, his only son, as a sacrifice, "even though God had said to him, 'It is through Isaac that your offspring will be reckoned'" (vv. 18–19).

- Isaac "blessed Jacob and Esau in regard to their future" in the midst of deception from his wife and son (v. 20).

- Jacob, after a long separation from his beloved son Joseph, "when he was dying, blessed each of Joseph's sons" (v. 21).

- Joseph, without experiencing it, "spoke about the [future] exodus of the Israelites from Egypt" (v. 22).

- Moses "chose to be mistreated along with the people of God rather than to enjoy the pleasures of sin for a short time. He regarded disgrace for the sake of Christ as of greater value than the treasures of Egypt...left Egypt...he persevered because he saw him who is invisible...he kept the Passover and the sprinkling of blood, so that the death angel would not touch the firstborn of Israel" (vv. 24–28).

- The Israelites "passed through the Red Sea as on dry land; but when the Egyptians tried to do so, they were drowned" (v. 29).

- The people marched around the walls of Jericho for seven days until the walls fell (v. 30).

- Rahab, who welcomed the spies, "was not killed with those who were disobedient" (v. 31).

And there were other heroes of the faith. Hebrews 11:32–38 speaks of them:

> And what more shall I say? I do not have time to tell about Gideon, Barak, Samson, Jephthah, David, Samuel and the

prophets, who through faith conquered kingdoms, administered justice, and gained what was promised; who shut the mouths of lions, quenched the fury of the flames, and escaped the edge of the sword; whose weakness was turned to strength; and who became powerful in battle and routed foreign armies. Women received back their dead, raised to life again. Others were tortured and refused to be released, so that they might gain a better resurrection. Some faced jeers and flogging, while still others were chained and put in prison. They were stoned; they were sawed in two; they were put to death by the sword. They went about in sheepskins and goatskins, destitute, persecuted and mistreated—the world was not worthy of them. They wandered in deserts and mountains, and in caves and holes in the ground.

Life wasn't trouble free and satisfying for any of these heroes. "These were all commended for their faith, yet none of them received what had been promised" (v. 39). But would they say it was worth it all? Indeed, that's exactly what the writer of Hebrews asserts in the final verse of that great chapter: "God had planned something better for us so that only together with us would they be made perfect" (v. 40).

What can we learn from their experiences that will prepare us to stand trial? We learn:

- Trials are not the exception in life. They are the rule!

- God allows trials to touch our lives in order to purify us.

- God's kingdom rule may even require that we lay down our very lives. Dying for Christ's sake (martyrdom) is the price some believers must pay for the kingdom.

- Our trials develop a sensitivity that helps us more effectively pray for others.

- We can trust our Father when facing trials.

In many parts of the world today, Christian converts expect to suffer trials. Each of us can expect to be brought to trial from time to time. Life is seasonal. No one is exempt from Satan's attack. No one is *always* victorious. Each of us will experience both defeat and victory in the spiritual trials we face.

LOSING EVERYTHING

"You don't realize that God is all you need, until God is all you've got!" It may not be good grammar, but it's true.

We had been married a couple of years when we pulled our new motor home into a Target shopping center in South Houston, Texas. We were in town to conduct a revival at Braeburn Valley Baptist Church.

Our motor home was not a luxury item. It represented everything we owned. We had no apartment or home. We lived in the motor home and traveled from church to church, week after week, conducting revival meetings and evangelistic crusades. You might say that we lived on a piece of "wheel estate" (pun intended)!

Alice had some light shopping to do prior to the evening service. I (Eddie) agreed to stay in the motor home, parked near the store's entrance.

As Alice shopped, I remembered that we also needed a can of hairspray. Knowing it would only take a couple of minutes for me to retrieve the hairspray and return to the motor home, I left the motor running and stepped into the store.

Sure enough, it was no problem at all. There was hardly anyone in the checkout line. In mere moments I was finished and walking toward the front door. As I exited the store I could hardly believe my eyes. It was like one of those disappearing African elephant or space shuttle illusions we have seen television magicians performing. Our motor home was gone. I actually saw it crossing the overpass and heading down the frontage road on the opposite side of the freeway.

I stepped back inside the store and walked over to the checkout stand. As Alice walked up I said, "Honey, are you looking for a good reason to praise the Lord?"

She smiled and answered good-naturedly, "Why, I don't need a *reason* to praise the Lord." Then I explained what had happened.

She could hardly believe her ears! "What are we going to do?" she asked.

"First, we'll call the police," I explained. "Then I'll call a taxi, because we have to get to the church for the evening service."

"Evening service? I'm dressed in slacks (in the early 1970s, women didn't wear slacks to church), and you're not dressed for church at all," Alice explained.

"We'll simply have to explain our situation to the people," I replied.

The taxi pulled up, and we left the Target store for the church. We told the curious driver what had just happened. He was baffled by our trust in the Lord. The conversation quickly shifted as our driver was confronted with his own relationship with God. When we arrived at the church, we had the joy of praying with him to receive Christ as his personal Lord and Savior.

That night, the service went on as usual. But we were numb. The people were very gracious to us. One family opened their home for us to sleep. Another bought us each a toothbrush. That night all we owned were the clothes on our backs and our new toothbrushes! As we prayed before a much-needed night's rest, we asked the Lord for understanding.

The days following were difficult. The police could not

report the crime as grand theft because our motor home's value did not exceed $50,000. The motor home was so new (only two weeks) that we hadn't even received the title in the mail. Since our motor home had only a temporary license plate, it could be easily replaced. Witnesses testified that two men were involved. The police offered us little encouragement. They said the thieves would likely take it across the Texas-Mexican border and sell it in Mexico for pennies on the dollar. However, God was our defender, and we asked Him to fight the battle for us.

When we weren't traveling, we stayed with friends and family, but when we traveled, hotels were our home. We had enough money to buy only basic items, and for a long time we ministered in the same two outfits each week. The generosity of God's people was what we remember the most.

One week turned into two, and two weeks turned into three. There was still no word from the police. Without any word on our motor home, our optimism turned to weeks of dying to self. Death to self came in several ways.

- Death to the gratification that owning "things" once gave us. It was not easy to release pictures, clothing and sentimental items. But it was necessary.

- Death to the opinions of others. What would people say? Do they think this has happened to us because we have sinned?

- Death to our need to be the master of our own fate. There is a mind-set permeating American society that says we can and should control life's circumstances.

Six weeks later, after we had surrendered everything to the Lord, we received a phone call from the police. The authorities found our empty motor home in a rice field east of Houston, buried up to its axles in mud. The crooks had stolen everything they considered to be of value. They burned everything else in a bonfire beside the motor home. The only things left undestroyed were our Bibles–neatly stacked under the kitchen table. The thieves were never found.

At the time God was working more on our *holiness* than our *happiness*. But we weren't the first to suffer. Nor was that the last suffering we have been called upon to endure. That's why Peter said, "Dear friends, do not be surprised at the painful trial you are suffering, as though something strange were happening to you" (1 Pet. 4:12).

Can any good thing come out of our trials? Well, read the following.

> Paul's sweetest epistles were written from prison; John's Revelation was written while he was in exile; Bunyan wrote *Pilgrim's Progress* while in Bedford jail; Luther translated the Bible into German while incarcerated in Wartburg Castle; Madame Guyon's sweetest poems and deepest experiences were the result of her long imprisonment. Truly, "Stone walls do not a prison make, nor iron bars a cage."[2]

THE ADVOCATES

Trouble is not strange. It's part of the natural process of life. God forges his finest tools in the fires of adversity. Knowing this, however, is sometimes little comfort when we are the ones in the furnace! For that reason, each one who is suffering adverse circumstances needs representation before the throne of God.

Prior to Simon Peter's infamous triple denial of Jesus, Jesus said to him, "Simon, Simon, Satan has asked to sift you as wheat. But I have prayed for you, Simon, that your faith may not fail. And when you have turned back, strengthen your brothers" (Luke 22:31–32). Jesus was assuring Peter that although he was about to be put on trial, he was not without representation in heaven's court. Jesus was committing to "stand in the gap" on Peter's behalf. It's clear that the Father did hear and answer Jesus' petition on Peter's behalf, because Peter's faith did not fail. In fact, Peter was so strengthened by his trial that he became a pillar of the early church. As Jesus had prophesied, Peter later strengthened his brothers by writing the words, "Do not be surprised at the painful trial you are suffering..." (1 Pet. 4:12).

When you engage in intercessory prayer, as Jesus did for Peter, in effect you become a spiritual defense attorney. You are pleading the case of another in heaven's court before Father God. What an awesome privilege and profound responsibility we assume when we do so! In this book we hope to challenge you with the indispensable nature of intercessory prayer.

Most earthly lawyers work either as defense attorneys or prosecuting attorneys, not as both. However, when we pray against the work of Satan and his militia in this world, we shift from serving as defense attorneys and begin operating from the position of a prosecuting attorney. Satan is no longer focusing on stealing, killing and destroying others. He suddenly finds himself a defendant in heaven's court. He is the one who is being tried! By God!

Surely you can see how important it is that we clearly understand our role and faithfully accept our responsibility to pray—and sometimes to fight when lives literally hang in the balance. The future depends on it.

In his devotional "Standing Up for Others," David Bryant, chairman of America's National Prayer Committee, writes:

> During and after the Vietnam War, many Americans wore pieces of jewelry called "MIA (Missing in Action) bracelets." Each person who wore a bracelet was an advocate for those in enemy hands who could not be

advocates for themselves...God intends that by our prayers, and out of our love for others, we reason with Him about their destiny.

Exodus 28:29 gives us a biblical illustration of advocacy prayer. Every time the high priest came into the tabernacle, on his vestment he bore across his heart the names of the tribes of Israel, inscribed on twelve stones. Like the MIA bracelet, these stones were a constant remembrance before the Lord (and to the priest) that the Israelites had no hope unless God acted on their behalf.

When we gather to pray, we, too, need to come wearing on our hearts, as it were, names of those around us for whom God has given us personal responsibility in prayer. We love them through prayer as we plead for them the way we would for any loved one who was trapped in prison. As advocates for others in prayer, we cry out to God for them: "They need what You have to give them, so I'm praying for those who cannot yet pray for themselves."[3]

Consider this a "handbook" that we have compiled to equip you for the challenge. In this book you will:

- Learn that faithfully enduring life's trials is your credentials for pleading the cases of others in prayer.

- Learn that every intercessor is a spiritual attorney, sometimes prosecuting the enemy but most of the time defending others.

- Learn the nature of heaven's courtroom.

- Discover the tactics of Satan (your adversary in court).

- Learn how to prepare both yourself and the cases that you will plead.

- Learn how to prevail in court and win favorable decisions on behalf of your clients (those for whom you are praying).

- Learn the difference between purpose-driven prayer and problem-centered praying.

Believe it! Once you have journeyed through this book with us, your prayer life will never be the same again! Now, let's take a look at a defense attorney named Job, perhaps earth's earliest-known advocate!

Do not pray for easy lives, pray to be stronger men.
Do not pray for tasks equal to your powers, pray for
powers equal to your task.
—Phillips Brooks

Chapter 2

Job's School
of Suffering

*Don't pray when you feel like it. Have an appointment with
the Lord and keep it. A man is powerful on his knees.*
—CORRIE TEN BOOM

THE crisp, cold morning air stings our lungs as we struggle to traverse the stony, briar-filled path toward the mountain's summit. The sun's rays are just beginning to peek over the horizon when suddenly the silence is pierced by a cry of agony. It's not a cry of pain. It's a cry of prayer. Even now we can almost hear Job praying.

The unknown author of the ancient Book of Job begins the book by introducing us to Job, the main character. Job was a blameless and upright man who feared God and hated evil. (See Job 1:1.) He is said to have been the greatest man among the people of the East.

Job was an intercessory advocate for his children. Early each morning Job would go to God on their behalf. Faithfully he sacrificed burnt offerings for them, thinking, *Perhaps my children have sinned and cursed God in their hearts* (Job 1:5). In effect he was fervently interceding in prayer, pleading their cases before the very throne of God as a defense attorney might plead their cases in court.

We don't find the word *advocate* in the Old Testament. We do, however, find instances of advocacy. For example, Abraham interceded with God for the city of Sodom (Gen. 18:23–33); Moses pled the case of the Israelites with God in prayer (Exod. 32:11–14); Samuel stood in the gap for the children of Israel (1 Sam. 7:8–9). Other examples of advocacy can be found in Jeremiah 14:7–9, 13, 19–22; Ezekiel 8 and Amos 7:2, 5–6.

One day as the angels presented themselves to the Lord, Satan entered Judge Jehovah's courtroom with them. The Lord asked Satan where he had been. He explained that he had been "roaming through the earth and going back and forth in it" (Job 1:7). Here, in Satan's own words, is his admission that he, unlike God, is not omnipresent.

Of course God knew what Satan had been up to. Thousands of years later the apostle Peter would explain, "Be self-controlled and alert. Your enemy the devil prowls around like a roaring lion looking for someone to devour" (1 Pet. 5:8). As a hungry lion scans the herd looking for the weak and the lame, Satan was scouring the earth for someone to victimize. God was well aware of his tactics.

The Judge, always the master strategist, was laying a subtle trap for His archenemy when He asked Satan, "Have you considered my servant Job? There is no one on earth like him; he is blameless and upright, a man who fears God and shuns evil'" (Job 1:8).

God knows His enemy's strengths and weaknesses. Satan's greatest strength is also his greatest weakness. He is called "the accuser." (See Revelation 12:10.) Immediately he began to accuse Job. Satan unjustly questioned Job's integrity. He accused Job of selfishness by suggesting that Job loved and served God only because of God's blessings:

> Then Satan answered the LORD, "Does Job fear God for nothing? Have you not put a fence around him and his house and all that he has, on every side? You have blessed the work of his hands, and his possessions have increased in the land. But stretch out your hand now, and touch all that he has, and he will curse you to your face."
>
> —JOB 1:9–11, NRSV

NEWS HEADLINES:
DEFENDER BECOMES DEFENDANT!

In the length of three short Bible verses, Job, an effective and faithful defense attorney for his own children, becomes Job the defendant! It's a complete role reversal. Prepare yourself for a similar experience. There are times when we will be faithfully praying for friends who are going through trial, and then without warning, we are the ones on trial! Overnight, we are in need of advocacy ourselves! Let's learn from the experience of Job.

You may recall that God allowed Satan certain liberties with Job—short of taking his life. He lost his children, his wealth, his health and his friends. Job experienced a serious trial. Most of our trials are like Sunday school picnics by comparison. According to God's sovereign design, Job was to become an example to men and women throughout history. Job, it could be argued, suffered more than anyone other than our Savior. But Job did not lose his commitment to the God he loved!

Once we see how trials become our friends, we shouldn't falter in our commitment to the Lord, either. As traveling musicians, we used to sing "I've Got Confidence," Andraé Crouch's catchy song about Job.

> Job was sick, oh so long
> Till the flesh fell from his bones.
> His wife, cattle and children,
> Everything that he had was gone.
> But Job he never despaired.
> He knew that God still cared.
> Sleepless days and sleepless nights,
> Job said, Honey, that's all right...
> 'Cause I've got confidence.
> God is gonna see me through.
> No matter what the case may be,
> I know He's gonna fix it for me.[1]

Job lost his possessions and his health. His seven sons and three daughters were killed in a freakish windstorm (Job 1:19). His wife lost her confidence in the Lord and any respect she had for her husband. Mrs. Job, seeing her husband so distressed, eventually encouraged him to forget his integrity, to "curse God and die" (Job 2:9).

But one of the greatest losses to Job was the loss of relationships. Perhaps you have heard the expression "Job's friends."

Job's School of Suffering

Job's friends became a *burden* rather than a blessing. Those who should have been sensitive to his need and supportive in their actions only added to his burden. Interestingly, each of them represents a type of friend that no one wants when going through trial.

Let's look at Job's friends. Perhaps in them we will learn the behaviors to avoid when our friends are suffering trials. We can develop an earnest desire to become effective prayer advocates when others have walked away.

ELIPHAZ—JOB'S RELIGIOUS FRIEND

When Job needed loving, practical friends to assist and support him in his hour of need, his friend Eliphaz took the opportunity to be "superspiritual." A person with a religious spirit is always looking for an opportunity to assert himself over you to "pull religious rank."

As Job suffered the loss of every earthly possession and experienced the agony of having excruciatingly painful boils cover his entire body, Eliphaz took pride in the occasion to bring correction to Job. He said:

> Job, I know you're in a lot of pain right now, but if you could be patient with me for a minute, I'd like to have a word with you. You've offered counsel and encouragement to lots of troubled people in the past. And you've been the first to support those who have stumbled. But now you're stumbling. And it's obvious that you're discouraged and dismayed regarding the trouble that has come to you. Job, I know that you think you're a righteous man. But let me ask you a question: When have you ever heard of an innocent man being destroyed? Job, God spoke to me in a *vision* about you. He said, "Eliphaz, can a mere mortal be more righteous than God? Can a man be purer than his Maker?"
>
> —Adapted from Job 4:12–17

A person who has a religious spirit often becomes mystical and secretive in an attempt to appear more spiritual than others. Eliphaz did this. He told Job, "Now a thing was *secretly* brought to me." He gloated over his private revelation by saying, "My thoughts from the *visions* of the night came on me *deep* in my sleep." Unfortunately, Eliphaz was out of touch with the reality of Job's intense suffering. The unsettling truth about friends who manifest the "I can hear God better than you" syndrome is that many of them have never personally experienced the genuine breaking from God. People with a religious spirit speak out of their soulishness and not from true brokenness.

What was the result? Eliphaz's "religious spirit" was showing! Job didn't need *religion*. He needed *relationship*. He needed a listening ear, not a sermon. Job needed an intercessor, not an instructor. Eliphaz thought he was serving God, when in fact he was an unknowing pawn of Satan. When called to the witness stand to defend Job, he became a star witness for the prosecution instead. He brought more—not less—despair and discouragement to Job.

When we are suffering, may God deliver us from religious friends. Decide right now that when your friends are suffering, you will relate to them with compassion and empathy.

People are still looking for relationships with God and others today. The editor of a New York City magazine experienced what may be her most unusual interview when she called me (Eddie) one afternoon. She asked, "Is this Reverend Smith?"

"No, it's not," I teased dryly.

"I'm sorry, I was calling to interview Eddie Smith," she continued.

"That's me," I answered. "What can I do for you?"

"Well," she said, "I'm a bit confused. I understood that you are a minister."

"I am a minister," I admitted.

"Can one be a minister and not be 'a reverend'?" she asked.

"Sure," I answered as I continued the play on words. "I just told you, I am."

"Why are you not 'a reverend'?" she inquired.

"It's easy," I clarified. "I revere no man and ask no one to revere me."

A bit taken aback, she continued, "And just what religion are you?"

"I don't have a religion," I admitted, knowing she'd be even more confused.

"What?" she answered. "You are a reverend without a religion?"

"No. I'm *not* a reverend without a religion," I said.

"Why don't you have a religion?" she pressed.

"Because God hates religion," I calmly explained.

"Why, I thought *religion* was God's idea!" she said.

"No, ma'am," I explained. "God's idea is relationship."

There was a long poignant pause in the conversation. Then she broke the silence, saying sincerely, "Eddie, I wish you had a church in New York. I think I'd love to attend it."

Many people in our fast-paced high-tech world are desperately looking for a *relationship with God,* not just *religion.* This is especially true when they are faced with life's adversities.

BILDAD—JOB'S IDEALISTIC FRIEND

An *idealist* is defined as "one who adheres to philosophical theories of perfection, excellence and concepts of flawless morality." This may sound good, but real life isn't quite this pristine.

When suffering life's trials, we neither need religious, holier-than-thou friends to scold us, nor idealistic friends like Bildad to rebuke us. Hearing Job's explanation, Bildad replied, "Job, what you are saying about your situation is nothing but 'hot air.' Let's be honest, Job. God doesn't pervert justice. You know that your children died because of their sin. So, I think it's high time that you plead with God for your own life. If you are the righteous man that you think you are, He will restore your health and other losses. If history teaches us anything, it teaches us that God won't reject the righteous or bless the wicked" (adapted from Job 8).

Many Christians today have overlooked the powerful process of suffering and trials that God has designed to produce godliness in each of our lives. Let's not forget that Timothy says, "All that will live godly in Christ Jesus shall suffer persecution" (2 Tim. 3:12, KJV). If we overlook that process, when suffering befalls our friends, we are apt to assume it is God's judgment for sin. When trouble befalls us, we are apt to be totally confused. (Read 1 Peter 1:7–9; 2 Peter 1:3–10; 2:9; James 1:2–4).

The Christian journey could be charted this way.

- Salvation
- Separation
- Dedication
- Service

Serving Christ is the goal of many Christians. "After all," they say, "We're saved to serve." Wrong. Service is not God's goal for our lives. Remember, Jesus said, "I no longer call you servants, because a servant does not know his master's business. Instead, I have called you friends, for everything that I learned from my Father I have made known to you" (John 15:15).

The Christian journey continues on to . . .

- Suffering
- Godliness
- Discipling

God's goal for us is godliness! He is transforming us into His own image! Godly Christians have not bypassed brokenness.

And only a godly Christian can disciple others toward godliness.

An idealistic person tends to revert back to tradition. So Bildad says, "Ask the former generations and find out what their fathers learned" (Job 8:8). Many idealists embrace the past moves of God while resisting His present activity. The worst place in the world to be is the place where God was. Regarding Job's sufferings, Bildad had absolutely no compassion due to his own defective self-image and his mistaken view of God. Since idealists think adversity is a sure sign of misguided living, they can offer us little support.

Sometimes God, for His own reasons, allows an idealistic friend to add to our test. At times we all need false and idealistic concepts to be broken. Perhaps through an idealistic friend we can see our blindness and resolve to fully surrender our heart to God. (See Psalm 51:17.) Whatever happens during the trials of life, pay close attention so you won't become bitter or angry. Allow the Lord to purify you, because without trials there will be no triumphs.

ZOPHAR–JOB'S LEGALISTIC FRIEND

A person who lives a life of legalism adheres to a strict, literal and excessively religious moral code. The New Testament Pharisees were the legalists of their day. The Aramaic form of the Hebrew word *perushim* for *Pharisees* means "separated." The Pharisees were constantly monitoring themselves and others by the Levitical law. These traditionalists burdened the people with special washings before eating bread or washing after they returned from the market. Pharisees demanded fasting twice a week and extravagance with the tithe. Yet, Jesus scolded them when He said, "But you have neglected the more important matters of the law—justice, mercy and faithfulness" (Matt. 23:23).

No doubt the whole spirit of their religion was summed up in self-righteousness, not in confession of sin or humility. This was the kind of friend Job had in Zophar, the legalist!

Zophar said, "Job, why do you think you are always right? Oh, how I wish that God would tell you the truth about your situation. You're not as smart as you think you are, Job. Can you understand the mysteries of God? God's ways are higher than the heavens, deeper than the grave, longer than the earth and wider than the sea. So what can you possibly know? Can you oppose God? He knows deceitful and evil men when he sees them. Job, a nitwit can no more become wise than a donkey can become a man. If you repent and put away your sin, then God will remove your shame" (adapted from Job 11:2–15).

With friends like these, who needs enemies? By being a legalist, Zophar has passed a sentence of judgment on Job. A legalist holds people to the letter of the Law. Yet, James 2:10 tells us, "For whoever keeps the whole law and yet stumbles at just one point is guilty of breaking all of it."

Apparently there was no one to plead the case for Job. His wife and friends all testified against him in court! Thank God this was not the case with Fiorello LaGuardia, New York's famed mayor.

> One winter's night in 1935, it is told, Fiorello LaGuardia, the irrepressible mayor of New York, showed up at a night court in the poorest ward of the city. He dismissed the judge for the evening and took over the bench. That night a tattered old woman, charged with stealing a loaf of bread, was brought before him. She defended herself by saying, "My daughter's husband has deserted her. She is sick and her children are starving."
>
> The shopkeeper refused to drop the charges, saying, "It's a bad neighborhood, your honor, and she's got to be punished to teach other people a lesson."
>
> LaGuardia sighed. He turned to the old woman and said, "I've got to punish you; the law makes no exceptions.

Ten dollars or ten days in jail." However, even while pronouncing sentence, LaGuardia reached into his pocket, took out a ten-dollar bill and threw it into his hat with these famous words: "Here's the ten-dollar fine, which I now remit, and furthermore, I'm going to fine everyone in the courtroom fifty cents for living in a town where a person has to steal bread so that her grandchildren can eat. Mr. Bailiff, collect the fines and give them to the defendant."

The following day, a New York newspaper reported: "Forty-seven dollars and fifty cents was turned over to a bewildered old grandmother who had stolen a loaf of bread to feed her starving grandchildren. Making forced donations were a red-faced storekeeper, seventy petty criminals and a few New York policemen."[2]

Interestingly, in this story, the old woman's judge became her defense attorney. And so it is with us. Jesus Christ reflects Judge Jehovah's heart as He defends us continually in heaven's court (Heb. 7:25). So we too should pray for each other in the hour of trial.

Let's not allow ourselves to become "Job's friends." When our friends are going through trials, let's not be a religious Eliphaz, an idealistic Bildad or a legalistic, know-it-all Zophar who are out of touch with their own pain. Let's agree to be spiritual defense attorneys, those who come alongside to bring carefully prayed-over and gently presented godly counsel, loving support and encouragement.

NEWS HEADLINES: DEFENDANT BECOMES DEFENDER!

The day came when the gavel dropped in heaven's court, and Job was pronounced "not guilty." Satan had lost the case against Job. Job did not, as Satan charged, reject God as a result of his trial. The tables were completely turned.

When God finished the work He was doing in Job, He promoted him from the role of suffering defendant to that of defense attorney once again. "After the LORD had said these things to Job, he said to Eliphaz the Temanite, 'I am angry with you and your two friends, because you have not spoken of me what is right, as my servant Job has'" (Job 42:7). What a turnaround!

Job's friends had failed to defend him in his trial. They had criticized, mocked and accused him. His friends had not understood the process of trial. Under Satan's cross-examination in court they inadvertently served as witnesses for the prosecution. In so doing, they had even falsely accused God. Now the Court's judgment weighed heavily upon them. Judge Jehovah was about to pass sentence on them.

Then our merciful Judge gave Job's friends these surprising instructions:

> So now take seven bulls and seven rams and go to my servant Job and sacrifice a burnt offering for yourselves. My servant Job will pray for you, and I will accept his prayer and not deal with you according to your folly. You have not spoken of me what is right, as my servant Job has.
>
> —JOB 42:8

What was the result? "So Eliphaz the Temanite, Bildad the Shuhite and Zophar the Naamathite did what the Lord told them; and the Lord accepted Job's prayer" (Job 42:9).

No television drama can compare with this story line! Do you see it? *"My servant Job will pray for you."* Wow! The Judge gave Eliphaz, Bildad and Zophar a court-appointed attorney— Job! As their attorney, Job was to plead their cases in prayer. And Job was no novice! Having defended his children and stood trial himself, Job the intercessor would not be praying detached, unfeeling, lifeless, ineffective prayers.

- He understood the pain and agony someone experiences when standing trial.

- He knew the fear, the loneliness and the severity of facing trial without a godly support team.

- He would represent his friends well before the Judge of heaven.

Friend, the trials you have suffered, when understood in the context of God's overall purposes and properly applied, can be used to a kingdom advantage as you intercede for others who are standing trial today.

For Job's friends, the best part was that their victory was guaranteed *before* their case even came to trial! That's right... *guaranteed!* Judge Jehovah said to Job's wayward friends, "I will accept his (Job's) prayer and not deal with you according to your folly." Wow!

We received a credit card offer in the mail yesterday. On it were written these words: "Guaranteed Acceptance." Can you imagine God telling you to ask Him for anything and promising in advance to give it to you? We would say that God had confidence in Job!

Some might think that a judge's decisions are always made in the courtroom. At least, that's the way television judges make it appear. In many cases, as in this case, the judge decides the matter in his private chamber, in conference with the opposing attorneys. The courtroom experience is simply to announce the decision publicly. Remember, Christian, as we enter into the Judge's private chambers to pray, God rules.

As the following story illustrates, when God rules from heaven there will be a discernable, measurable manifestation of His decision "in the streets."

For years the city of Hong Kong, China, had a district that

was marked by violence, drugs, strife, fear, poverty, alienation and discrimination. It was the Pillar Point refugee camp at Tuen Mun. The camp was little more than a miserable prison for the refugee families—mostly Vietnamese—incarcerated there.

In the spring of 1999 several hundred Hong Kong pastors and intercessors attended the Spiritual Warfare and Spiritual Mapping Conference I (Alice) taught. Following the conference, I led a team of select pastors and intercessors to research and pray on site at Pillar Point—the site where Hong Kong's first inhabitants worshiped the stone goddess, the Queen of Heaven. The team repented on behalf of those first inhabitants who had worshiped demonic gods, for the harsh treatment of the Vietnamese refugees and for the sins committed at the Tuen Mun camp. We stood in the gap to pray.

Several days of violence erupted in the camp on the evening Eddie and I left Hong Kong to return home to the United States. The upheaval shook every level of government, even the policy makers. The Hong Kong prayer team saw this as a sign that God had heard and was going to answer them.

At midnight May 31, 2000, almost a year from the date that we prayer-walked Pillar Point, the refugee camp at Tuen Mun was closed, putting an end to this dark chapter in Hong Kong's recent history. We can look with expectancy for spiritual and physical change in Hong Kong.[3]

Our Father is the God of peace, not violence...of life, not death. We pleaded the case and the conditions of the Vietnamese people before the Father. The result was better living conditions for them. The refugees have been given government allowances and housing within the city of Hong Kong. The cases we effectively plead in heaven's court will result with physical manifestations.

JOB PASSES THE TEST

But exactly *when* was it that Job's circumstances changed? When did his personal victory come? Was it while Satan was stripping him of everything? No. Was it while he was complaining and debating with God? No. Three things were required in order for Job's situation to be resolved.

1. Job had to see and understand God in a new way.

Devastating adversity drove this devoted man to a deeper commitment to God. When adversity visits us, we have a choice. We can either allow the problem to move us closer to God, or we can resist and run. Job chose God. In spite of his obvious misfortune, rather than question God's integrity and faithfulness, Job wisely cast himself on the mercy of the Court. And once Job saw the glory of God, he was heard to say, "My ears had heard of you but now my eyes have seen you. Therefore I despise myself and repent in dust and ashes" (Job 42:5–6).

The Lord wants to reveal Himself to us in our trials, too. Job, the defendant in this case, had turned the corner, passed the test and completed the process God had designed. He had proven, once and for all, that no one's personal loss need destroy his relationship with God. (See Romans 8:38–39.) Job had proven what David also discovered—that distress can actually strengthen us if we remain true to the Lord (Ps. 4:1.)

2. Job had to see himself in a new light.

This dilemma caused Job to lose all confidence in the flesh. It is apparent from the text that this righteous man Job, more righteous than any of his peers, had an unacceptable level of self-esteem. Once he saw God as He really is, rather than the way he'd previously assumed God to be, Job acknowledged, "I despise myself and repent..." (Job 42:6). God's humiliation of Job resulted in a new level of humility.

The Lord doesn't want to humiliate us. But He will if we refuse to humble ourselves, because He resists the proud and gives grace to the humble (James 4:6). So, like Job, we can refuse to allow the trial to finish its work in us. Or, more wisely, we can look for God's purposes in our trials and embrace them wholeheartedly that we might be changed. We are not suggesting self-pity, but self-purity. When we are as committed to being personally transformed as we are to having our problems solved, God can demonstrate His miraculous power in our lives.

3. Job learned to see his relationship with others in a new way.

It was Jesus who taught us, "Love the Lord your God with all your heart and with all your soul and with all your mind and with all your strength . . . Love your neighbor as yourself." (Mark 12:30–31).

As long as Job remained the self-absorbed defendant, primarily concerned with his own need, he was a victim. It was only when he became a God-conscious, God-ordained, anointed defender of others that he experienced his own victory! "And the Lord turned the captivity of Job, when he prayed for his friends" (Job 42:10, KJV).

Yes, Job's captivity was turned when he *prayed for his friends.* When Job focused on God and others, *his own captivity* was turned!

Have you noticed how some of the best ministers to the suffering are those who once experienced suffering themselves? Many drug counselors once struggled against chemical addition themselves or shared the pain and tears of an addicted friend or family member. Many who were formerly abused work with the abused. God uses life's tragedies as building blocks when we love Him, submit to His purposes and place them in His hands. The apostle Paul wrote, "And we know that in all things God works for the good of those who love him, who have been called according to his purpose" (Rom. 8:28). In 2 Corinthians 5:17 he wrote, "Therefore, if anyone is in Christ, he is a new creation; the old has gone, the new has come!"

Some of us, perhaps even you, are trying to escape the pain of our past. We are trying to bury the hurtful things that we have experienced. We have not understood the ways of God. The gospel message is this:

- God makes the old new.

- Then He weaves together all that we have experienced into the tapestry of our lives.

- The result is that we become a beautiful work of art in His hands.

What we are saying is this. Those painful past experiences you have suffered, things that you thought were disqualifying factors in your life, are really your "credentials for ministry."

As Job's suffering prepared him to intercede for his friends, and the pain and suffering of Jesus' earthly trial was used by the Father to prepare Him to serve in our defense, so will God use our painful trials to prepare us for our role as prayer defendants. God is preparing us to plead the cases of others in prayer. Personal trauma has indeed trained many intercessors!

SAMUEL, THE LEPER

As I (Eddie) stepped outside the curio shop in Madras, the odorous blends of curry and cow dung hung heavily in the Asian air. Out of the corner of my eye, I noticed a pitiful beggar lying on a mat on the busy city sidewalk. People were walking around him, and bicycles and carts were dodging him. I looked again. He was a pathetic sight. Both of his legs, one of his arms, most of his hand and face were missing. He was a leper.

I moved closer to him. And as I looked deeper into his dark brown eyes I caught a glimpse of something familiar in his countenance. He had a peaceful, satisfied look. I instructed my interpreter, "Ask this man his name, and see if he is a Christian." Stopping the traffic momentarily, we knelt beside the man, and they spoke briefly in Hindi.

"His name is Samuel," he reported. "And yes, he is a believer!"

I asked if I could talk with Samuel. With the help of my interpreter I introduced myself to Samuel and asked, "Brother, where do you live?"

"I live with my sister, two blocks from here." Samuel answered as he smiled broadly.

"Are all of your needs met, Samuel?" I asked.

His face lit up as he assured me that they were. From the look on his face, you would have thought that his entire life had known nothing but God's favor. I reached into my pocket and pulled out a $20 U.S. bill and dropped it into his cup. He beamed with a sincere, but surprised look of gratitude. I stood again and looked through the store window for Alice and the rest of our team.

Unexpectedly, I suddenly felt a strong tug at my pants leg. It was Samuel. He had dragged his rubber pallet over to where I was standing. Using his remaining hand he was tenaciously trying to get my attention. Unfortunately, my interpreter had left. So with sign language I tried to tell him I couldn't understand him. Unrelenting, Samuel motioned for me to kneel beside him again. I knelt. Then the most remarkable thing occurred.

Samuel had noticed a small plastic Velcro brace on my forearm. My arm wasn't injured, but because of the heavy weight of our luggage, I was wearing the brace to prevent any muscle strain. As I knelt beside Samuel, he placed his good hand with his three remaining fingers on my arm brace, closed his eyes and began to pray fervently for my healing in his Hindi language.

Alice and the team could hardly believe their eyes as they

walked out into the sun. There I was, kneeling on the sidewalk as a leper prayed for my healing. Alice captured that remarkable moment on film. That day I learned a life-changing lesson that I want to share with you.

You may be waiting until your problems are solved, your healing is manifested, you get a better job or until you gain more experience before you begin ministering to the needs of others. Samuel's life of suffering had caused him to be sensitive to the needs of those around him. It would have been easy for him to overlook the apparent pain of someone like me. He could have sought to excuse himself from ministering to me because, by comparison, I was wealthier or healthier than he. Not Samuel. He had a different philosophy. Samuel figured, "If I have one good hand left, I can lay it on somebody and pray!" Why don't you adopt Samuel's ministry perspective today? There are plenty of people who need your hand laid on them in prayer. What are you waiting for?

Are you currently enrolled in "the school of suffering?" Perhaps you have been experiencing some Job-like trials of your own. When will they end? That's really the wrong question. The question we should ask is, "What will they produce?" And that, friend, is largely up to you. If you are facing trial today:

- Press in to the Lord, and make a commitment that your trials will not cause you to give up.

- Ask the Lord for a new personal revelation of Himself.

- Humble yourself before the great Judge of the nations.

- Then look for another person who needs a good defense attorney and become that person's advocate before the throne of God in prayer.

It could be that your captivity, like Job's, will be turned as you pray for your friends! Immerse yourself in *their* victory, and you will likely discover your own! "So the LORD blessed the latter end of Job more than his beginning" (Job 42:12, KJV). May this also be said of you!

In the next chapter we will examine our representation in heaven's courtroom.

If I could hear Christ praying for me in the
next room, I would not fear a million enemies.
Yet distance makes no difference. He is praying for me.
—ROBERT MURRAY MCCHEYNE

Chapter 3

Mr. Christian
Goes to Court

True prayer is born out of brokenness.
—Francis J. Roberts

AMERICA, we are a litigious society, a greedy culture. Too many of us are out to make a buck. And the easiest way to make money, other than winning the lottery, the Publishers' Clearing House Sweepstakes or *Who Wants to Be a Millionaire?*, is to win a lawsuit. Look at the following news headlines:

- Woman Awarded Millions in Settlement After Spilling Hot McDonald's Coffee in Her Lap

- Millions Awarded Man Who Caught His Ear on Subway Strap

- Lady Wins Huge Cash Settlement From Nike After Tripping Over Her Own Shoestring

A minister we know was sued for releasing an unfit worker from employment in his ministry. Another minister was sued for one million dollars because of an unfortunate and unavoidable bus accident on a mission trip. A dear pastor friend of ours was brought to trial, along with his church, for refusing to return a church member's past tithes. Today, churches, pastors and counselors are being burdened with heavy insurance premiums to protect themselves from litigation.

Perhaps you have not yet been sued in court. Consider yourself fortunate! However, you have not escaped Satan's charges against you. In the court of heaven, Satan continually brings accusation against every Christian. Why? Because Satan is God's archenemy, and he is determined to discredit God. Of course, he cannot discredit God directly regarding God's actions. So Satan attempts to discredit God indirectly, regarding our actions. That's why he tempts us to sin.

The writer of Hebrews wrote, "We have been made holy through the sacrifice of the body of Jesus Christ once for all...because by one sacrifice he has made perfect forever those who are being made holy" (Heb. 10:10, 14). These are complex and fascinating verses. Notice that verse 10 says that we *have been made* holy. Yet verse 14 says that we *are being made* holy. Which is it? Have we been made holy, or are we being made holy? The answer is...they are both true! We who are in Christ are *positionally* already made holy. For that reason, God can and does live within us. But, *experientially* we are being made holy. Paul wrote, "For those God foreknew he also predestined to be conformed to the likeness of his Son...And those he predestined, he also called; those he called, he also justified; those he justified, he also glorified" (Rom. 8:29–30). From God's positional perspective, our *glorification* as well as our salvation and sanctification are past tense. They are future history! We are in the process of becoming who we are!

These things may be difficult for us to grasp, but Satan understands God's plan and purpose. After all, he has known God far longer than any of us. Satan also understands us all too well. He has coexisted and interacted with generations of God's people. He knows that although we are already positionally perfected in the heart of God, we are working out our salvation from day to day (Phil. 2:12). Satan's evil intentions are to cause us to:

- Compromise our convictions
- Fall into sin
- Grieve the Holy Spirit
- Short-cycle God's plan to conform us into Christ's image

In essence, he wants to discredit God. The moment we slip, the devil will ruthlessly accuse us as he accused Job. The name *Satan* means "accuser." Not surprisingly then, Satan relentlessly accuses us day and night in the court of heaven. In so doing, he is accusing God of failing to complete what He started—our salvation. (See Philippians 1:6; Revelation 12:10.)

Through the years we have served on many jury panels. We have seen some excellent advocates at work. But in some cases, we have seen some pitiful representation. Believe us, when facing trial, there are few things more comforting than having experienced, effective legal representation.

When Satan accuses us in heaven's court we are fortunate to have a veteran attorney. In 1 John 2:1, John describes the courtroom:

> My dear children, I write this to you so that you will not sin.
> But if anybody does sin, we have one who speaks to the
> Father in our defense—Jesus Christ, the Righteous One.
> —1 JOHN 2:1

As Abraham, Moses and others petitioned the cases of sinners in the Old Testament, Jesus, our attorney, intercedes with the Father on behalf of sinners. However, Jesus Christ (the Righteous) is not only our High Priest—He is also our atoning Sacrifice!

The King James Version says, "We have an advocate with the Father." The writer, John, uses the Greek word *parakletos* to describe Jesus as an *advocate*. The same word is used in John's Gospel in chapters 15 and 16 to describe the Holy Spirit. In both passages the word *parakletos* means "advocate or attorney." Another primary meaning of the word is "intercessor." Yes, intercessor! The Holy Spirit and Jesus share the roles of *attorney* and *intercessor* for us!

This verse uniquely implies that when we sin, we are brought to trial before God. Jesus Christ is our defense attorney; He will be pleading our case. And what a defense attorney He is!

CHARACTERISTICS OF OUR ATTORNEY

He has impeccable qualifications.

Jesus Christ's credentials are completely unattainable by

human means. He is none other than Jesus Christ, the Righteous! And it's a good thing, for to be effective in the court of heaven, righteousness is of prime importance! James wrote, "The prayer of a righteous man [or woman] is powerful and effective" (James 5:16).

In September of 1977, during the pre-Christmas season in Moline, Illinois, Terry Schafer had a special gift she wanted to purchase for her husband, David. She feared her choice was too expensive. Oh, it wouldn't be too expensive for some families, but when you have to make ends meet on a policeman's salary, this could be too expensive. The gift was on her mind as she wandered along Fifth Avenue, hoping to find something like it—or perhaps the very thing she had in mind—at a price she could afford.

Sure enough, she spotted the very thing. She slipped into the store and chatted casually with the kind shopkeeper for a few minutes. She mentioned that she was looking for the perfect gift for her policeman husband. Then she looked into his eyes and asked, "How much?"

"$127.50," he replied.

Ouch. Her anticipation turned to disappointment as she thought, *That's just too much for us. We can't afford it.* And then an idea popped into her mind. She said to the shopkeeper, "Though we don't know each other, perhaps you would allow me to put it on hold. I can pay a little down payment now. Then about the end of October, I'll come back and pay you more. I promise you, by the time you have it gift-wrapped before Christmas, I'll pay the last amount."

A seasoned businessman, he knew a soul who could be trusted when he saw one. So he smiled and said, "I'll tell you what. Because your husband is a police officer, I have every reason to trust you. Why don't you just give me the first pay-ment? I'll gift-wrap it and let you take it with you today." She was elated. She walked out with this wonderful gift she was so anxious to give to her husband.

But like a lot of us, she wasn't able to keep the secret. So that night as David unwrapped the gift, Terry stood there beaming. He was thrilled at her thoughtfulness and covered her with hugs and kisses. Neither one of them realized, however, how significant that simple gift was. As a matter of fact, in the not-too-distant future, it would be the difference between David's life and death.

On October 1 of that same year, Patrolman David Schafer was working the night shift when he received a call on his police radio. A drugstore robbery was in process. Racing to the scene, he arrived just in time to observe the suspect getting into his car, starting the engine and speeding away. Quickly David switched on his siren and began the pursuit. Three blocks later the getaway vehicle suddenly pulled over to the side of the road and stopped.

The suspect was still seated behind the wheel of his car as David cautiously approached the vehicle. About three feet from the driver's door, it flew open and the suspect fired an automatic pistol once, sending a .45-caliber slug toward David's stomach.

At seven o'clock the next morning, Terry answered the door of the Schafer's home. Carefully and calmly, the police officer explained David had been shot while trying to apprehend a robbery suspect. As the officer detailed what happened to David, he had bad news and good news. As she listened to the details of what had happened, Terry Schafer thought how glad she was that she didn't wait until Christmas to give her gift to her husband. She was grateful for the kind shopkeeper who had been willing to let her pay for it later. Otherwise, David Schafer, shot at point-blank range with a deadly .45-caliber pistol, would surely have died. But the good news was that he was alive and in the hospital—not with a gunshot wound, but with a deep bruise in his abdomen.

Christmas had come early that year, and David had worn the gift of life his wife could not wait to give—his brand-new bulletproof vest.

That's why Christ came. He came to give us a vest of righteousness, to pay the price with His blood that He might protect us with a shield that sin could never penetrate.[1]

He has superior intelligence.

Jesus Christ our attorney *is God.* John reports, "In the beginning was the Word, and the Word was with God, and the Word was God" (John 1:1). As God, He is *omniscient.* He knows all things! That, friend, is *superior intelligence!*

The book *Disorder in the Court* includes actual statements by lawyers recorded during court proceedings. As you read some of these statements below, we believe they will prove how important it is that one's attorney be qualified and intelligent.

> *Attorney:* Doctor, how many autopsies have you performed on dead people?
> *Witness:* All my autopsies are performed on dead people.
> *Attorney:* Do you recall the time that you examined the body?
> *Witness:* The autopsy started around 8:30 P.M.
> *Attorney:* And Mr. Dennington was dead at the time?
> *Witness* (in sarcasm): No, he was sitting on the table wondering why I was doing an autopsy on him!
> *Attorney:* Doctor, before you performed the autopsy, did you check for a pulse?
> *Witness:* No.
> *Attorney:* Did you check for blood pressure?
> *Witness:* No.
> *Attorney:* Did you check for breathing?
> *Witness:* No.

Attorney: So, then it is possible that the patient was alive when you began the autopsy?
Witness: No.
Attorney: How can you be so sure, Doctor?
Witness: Because his brain was sitting on my desk in a jar.
Attorney (grasping for straws): But could the patient still have been alive nevertheless?
Witness: Yes, it is possible that he could have been alive and practicing law somewhere![2]

(Hello! Anyone home? What was this attorney thinking?)

He has knowledge of the law.

Jesus Christ, our lawyer "cuts no corners." He does everything "by the Book." And why not? After all, *He wrote the Book!* So, He will never be caught off guard in the courtroom. And, being God, unlike human judges, His decisions are final.

Justice Gray of the Supreme Court once said to a man who appeared before him in a lower court and escaped penalty by some technicality, "I know that you are guilty, and I wish you to remember that one day you will stand before a better and wiser Judge. There you will be dealt with according to the law of God."[3]

He has experience.

Jesus our attorney is no novice. He is highly experienced. First, He is Himself a graduate of the School of Suffering. (See chapter 2.) One day Jesus was brought to trial before Pilate, the Roman governor. Pilate asked him, "Are you the King of the Jews?"

Jesus replied, "Yes, I am."

The leading priests and the older Jewish leaders accused Jesus of not paying taxes and for claiming to be the Christ...a king. They continued to taunt Him, but He refused to answer them.

Mr. Christian Goes to Court

So Pilate asked Jesus franticly, "Don't You hear these people accusing You of all these things?"

To Pilate's surprise Jesus said nothing.

Pilate suspected that the accusations stemmed from anger, malice, unfounded jealousy... nothing but lies—but what could he do?

While he was judging Jesus, Pilate's wife sent him a message saying, "Don't do anything to that man. He is not guilty. Today I had a distressing dream about Him."

Confused and concerned, Pilate asked the people, "What should I do with Jesus, the one who is called Christ?"

In unison the crowd roared, "Kill Him!"

Pilate pleaded, "Why should I kill Him... for what? He's done nothing wrong."

But again they thundered, "Kill Him!"

When Pilate saw that the angry mob was on the verge of rioting, he washed his hands in front of them and said, "I am not guilty of this man's death. You are the ones who are causing it!"

Frenzied by lying spirits, the crowd answered, "We will be responsible. We accept for ourselves and for our children any punishment for His death."

In his frustration, Pilate ordered his soldiers to whip Jesus. Arrogantly they took Him into the governor's palace where they stripped Him and tied a purple robe to His back. They twisted thorny branches into a crown and beat it into His tender scalp until the blood ran down His face. In a demonic rage, the Roman soldiers plucked out Jesus' beard and whipped His back with thirty-nine lashes until the flesh lay loose from His body. They thrust a stick into Jesus' hand, bowed down to Him and yelled mockingly, "Hail, King of the Jews!"

Unrelenting, the soldiers spat on Jesus, jerked the stick from His hand and continued to beat Him in the face. When they finished their fun, the bloodthirsty men took off the robe, redressed

Jesus and led Him away to be nailed to a cross. Scripture reports that Jesus was so marred from this torture that many were astounded. He was unrecognizable; no man had ever endured suffering like His. (Paraphrased from Isaiah 50:6; 52:13–15; 53:3–8; Matthew 26:67–68; Mark 15:16–23; Luke 22:63–65.)

But this was not the first time Jesus was brought to trial! Perhaps you remember the day when Jesus stood trial before His own disciples—and, ostensibly, the whole earth:

> When Jesus came to the region of Caesarea Philippi, he asked his disciples, "Who do people say the Son of Man is?"
>
> They replied, "Some say John the Baptist; others say Elijah; and still others, Jeremiah or one of the prophets."
>
> "But what about you?" he asked. "Who do you say I am?"
>
> Simon Peter answered, "You are the Christ, the Son of the living God."
>
> Jesus replied, "Blessed are you, Simon son of Jonah, for this was not revealed to you by man, but by my Father in heaven."
>
> —MATTHEW 16:13–17

Jesus was clearly on trial that day as well. In one sense, Planet Earth was a courtroom where Jesus lived His entire life on trial. The primary issue was His true identity. Who was this man Jesus? Was He who He claimed to be? Isaiah writes of Him, "He was despised and rejected by men, a man of sorrows, and familiar with suffering. Like one from whom men hide their faces he was despised, and we esteemed him not. Surely he took up our infirmities and carried our sorrows, yet we considered him stricken by God, smitten by him, and afflicted" (Isa. 53:3–4). Our Savior was:

- Despised
- Rejected
- Familiar with sorrow

- Familiar with suffering
- Not esteemed by others
- Stricken and smitten by God
- Afflicted

Not surprisingly then, Jesus is our defense attorney, our intercessor who bears our grief and carries our sorrows when we are brought to trial.

The second area of experience Jesus brings to the courtroom is His proven advocacy skills. After all, His life and ministry were permeated with personal prayer.

- He pleaded the children's case—Matthew 19:13–14
- He pleaded Simon Peter's case—Luke 22:32
- He pleaded for Lazarus—John 11:41–42
- He pleaded the case of His disciples—John 17:9
- He even pleaded our case before ascending into heaven—John 17:20

Having accomplished all that He was sent to do, Jesus Christ ascended into heaven's courtroom to continue His legal career by pleading our future cases. Paul, describing Jesus' current role, wrote: "Who will bring any charge against those whom God has chosen? It is God who justifies. Who is he that condemns? Christ Jesus, who died—more than that, who was raised to life—is at the right hand of the Father and is also interceding for us" (Rom. 8:33–34).

He has divine connections.

Our attorney is the Judge's Son. You talk about influence in the courtroom—the Judge is His Daddy! In fact, the Judge publicly announced of Him one day, "This is my Son, whom I love; with him I am well pleased" (Matt. 3:17). As if to underscore this, Jesus said, "The one who sent me is with me; he has not left me alone, for I always do what pleases him" (John 8:29).

Bruce Lockerbie, in his book *Fatherlove,* tells this story.

> When I was just eleven years old, our family drove from
> Toronto to Eastern Ontario to the region north of the St.
> Lawrence River where my father had been born. We
> reached the little villages of Ventnor and Spencerville just
> before midnight. The residents had long since gone to
> bed. But Dad needed directions to find the old home-
> stead where we were to spend the night. Reluctantly he
> stopped at a darkened house and knocked on the door.
> After several minutes of waiting, the yard light came on,
> and an older man opened the door. I could hear my father
> apologizing for the inconvenience; and then he identified
> himself as the son of Pearson Lockerbie—my grandfather,
> dead for more than a score of years.
>
> "Oh, come in, come in," said the old man. "No trouble
> at all. We knew your father."…That's the greatest legacy
> a man can leave his son.[4]

He has a sterling reputation.

Another great advantage our attorney has over any other is
His superior name. Paul writes of Jesus, "Therefore God exalted
him to the highest place and gave him the name that is above
every name, that at the name of Jesus every knee should bow, in
heaven and on earth and under the earth" (Phil. 2:9–10).

We like the story about a young musician's concert that
was poorly received by the critics. The famous Finish com-
poser Jean Sibelius consoled him by patting him on the
shoulder and saying, "Remember son, there is no city in the
world where they have erected a statue to a critic."[5]

Yes, critics throughout the world have questioned the reputation of Jesus, but remember He has perfect standing in both
heaven and earth!

He is on call twenty-four hours a day.

Jesus our advocate—our attorney, our heavenly lawyer—is on a permanent retainer and is always accessible! "Therefore he is able to save completely those who come to God through him, because he *always lives to intercede* for them" (Heb. 7:25, emphasis added). The psalmist reminds us, "He who watches over you will not slumber; indeed, he who watches over Israel will neither slumber nor sleep" (Ps. 121:3–4).

He represents us *pro bono* (for free).

Because we are His, there are no fees! Hallelujah! When we sin, Jesus pleads our case at no charge to us. Jesus paid it all! (See 1 John 2:2.)

A cartoon in the *New Yorker* magazine showed an exasperated father saying to his prodigal son, "This is the fourth time we've killed the fatted calf." Jesus freely represents us over and over in our lifetime. Aren't we glad?[6]

HEAVEN'S COURTROOM

Looking around this vast courtroom, we are awed by the expanse. It appears that everything revolves around the Judge's throne in the center of the room. He is Judge Jehovah, the Creator and the great I AM.

It is difficult for us to make out His features, but the Judge has the appearance of precious stones, and an emerald colored rainbow encircles Him (Rev. 4:1–3).

Daniel gives us another view of the Judge. He writes:

> As I looked, thrones were set in place, and the Ancient of Days took his seat. His clothing was as white as snow; the hair of his head was white like wool. His throne was flaming with fire, and its wheels were all ablaze. A river of fire was flowing, coming out from before him. Thousands upon thousands attended him; ten thousand times ten

thousand stood before him. The court was seated, and the books were opened.

—DANIEL 7:9–10

Around the Judge's bench are twenty-four other thrones upon which are seated twenty-four elders. Each is dressed in white and wears a golden crown. One can't help but wonder who these elders are and what measure of service has qualified each to sit in his lofty eternal position (Rev. 4:4).

Wow! What was that? It was a flash of brilliant light, a rumble of thunder that sounded like a million waterfalls and a tumultuous crack of lightning! This place is awesome!

Circling above the Judge's head are four unearthly creatures. They are definitely extraterrestrial! One creature has the face of a lion; another has the face of a man. The next has a face of an eagle, and the fourth the face of an ox. Each creature has six wings! Moving closer we notice that each has eyes all over its body, even under its wings.

As strange as they look to us, it is not their appearance that captures our attention but rather their cries. They apparently have only one job. They shout a single proclamation over and over and over again. Listen... there it is!

> Holy, holy, holy is the Lord God Almighty, who was, and is, and is to come.
>
> —REVELATION 4:8

Endlessly they repeat this heavenly mantra.

Amazing! Did you see that? When the four creatures cried out, the twenty-four elders fell rather unceremoniously from their seats and upon their faces on the crystal floor. They slid their crowns off their heads and pushed them toward the throne saying, "You are worthy, our Lord and God, to receive glory and honor and power, for you created all things, and by your will they were created and have their being" (Rev. 4:11).

What is that beautiful song that we hear in the background? We are beginning to see something through the cloud of incense that seems to be rising from the earth. It is some sort of huge choir, and they are singing these words: "Worthy is the Lamb, who was slain, to receive power and wealth and wisdom and strength and honor and glory and praise!" (Rev. 5:12).

Next to the Judge's bench sits another authority. He is a blend of majesty and mercy. He is kingly and yet has the appearance of a lamb. And the awful scars...My, what suffering He must have endured (Rev. 5:6).

What a contrast between this courtroom and the courtrooms of earth. Everything here is so perfect. The only imperfections found here are those scars. They are the only works of men's hands.

Multiplied millions of beings surround the throne, the Lamb and the elders:

> Then I looked and heard the voice of many angels, numbering thousands upon thousands, and ten thousand times ten thousand. They encircled the throne and the living creatures and the elders. In a loud voice they sang: "Worthy is the Lamb, who was slain, to receive power and wealth and wisdom and strength and honor and glory and praise!" Then I heard every creature in heaven and on earth and under the earth and on the sea, and all that is in them, singing: "To him who sits on the throne and to the Lamb be praise and honor and glory and power, for ever and ever!" The four living creatures said, "Amen," and the elders fell down and worshiped.
> —Revelation 5:11–14

There is another multitude surrounding the throne in that great courtroom. It is the great host of saints!

> After this I looked and there before me was a great multi-
> tude that no one could count, from every nation, tribe,
> people and language, standing before the throne and in
> front of the Lamb. They were wearing white robes and
> were holding palm branches in their hands. And they
> cried out in a loud voice: "Salvation belongs to our God,
> who sits on the throne, and to the Lamb."
>
> —REVELATION 7:9–10

Included in that great throng of saints are some of our loved ones! This throng fills the gallery in heaven and witnesses the power of the prayers of the saints (Rev. 5:8; 8:3–5.)

But just as these witnesses fill the courtroom in what the Bible calls the "third heaven" (2 Cor. 12:1–4), so too there are witnesses in the second heaven where Satan, "the ruler of the kingdom of the air," lives (Eph. 2:2). In Ephesians 6:12, God says that "the rulers, the authorities, the powers of this dark world and the spiritual forces of evil in the heavenly realms" are learning as they witness our living. "His [God's] intent was that now, through the church, the manifold wisdom of God should be made known to the rulers and authorities in the heavenly realms, according to his eternal purpose which he accomplished in Christ Jesus our Lord" (Eph. 3:10–11).

WITNESSES HERE

As there are witnesses in the galleries of the second heaven, the world also watches us. We are teaching them whether or not we consider prayer important and effective.

Prayer was very important to Jesus—and His disciples knew that it was. "One day Jesus was praying in a certain place. When he finished, one of his disciples said to him, 'Lord, teach us to pray'" (Luke 11:1). Is prayer so important to your success in life that those around you want to learn to pray in the same way that you pray?

Mr. Christian Goes to Court

It is interesting, isn't it, that the disciples didn't ask Jesus to teach them how to heal the sick, raise the dead, walk on water or deliver the captives. They apparently knew that the key to those things would be found in His life of prayer.

Satan is the prosecutor, and we are the defendants who are to overcome him by the blood of Jesus. "They overcame him by the blood of the Lamb and by the word of their testimony; they did not love their lives so much as to shrink from death" (Rev. 12:11).

The following imaginary story will help to illustrate the action as each case is presented in that heavenly courtroom.

When Mr. Christian sins, Satan the prosecutor runs breathlessly into heaven's courtroom with a digital picture of the event (Job 1:6–7).

"Your Honor," he charges sarcastically, "I would like to place into court's evidence this photo of your servant, Mr. Christian. It clearly shows him running a stop sign in his automobile."

The bailiff takes the photo and hands it to the Father, who examines it carefully. Then Judge Jehovah turns to the advocate, Jesus Christ the Righteous, and asks, "My Son, how do You plead this case?"

It would appear that Jesus is at a disadvantage. If He pleads Mr. Christian's guilt, then the defendant has no hope of reaching heaven, for no sin can ever enter heaven. But if Jesus declares Mr. Christian's innocence, it would be a lie. Mr. Christian really did fail to stop at the sign. And Jesus never "cuts corners"!

He rubs His chin, thinks for a moment, then resolutely says to the Father, "Your Honor, I neither plead Mr. Christian's innocence nor his guilt. Rather, I choose to plead My blood!" A look of horror flashes across the prosecutor's face as he hears the words "My blood." Satan leaps from his comfortable chair, cups his hands over his ears, screams and runs out of the courtroom. He can't stand the thought of the blood of Jesus Christ.

Before Satan even reaches the door, the Judge's gavel crashes down upon the desk and His voice thunders, "Not guilty!" Not guilty, what comfort these words are to a sinner's ears.

Another story further helps us to understand the far-reaching effects of the "Not guilty!" verdict.

> Not long ago there died a benevolent doctor. It had been his custom, as he went through his books and saw this debt and that debt, one after the other, and realized that it was not paid because the patient could not pay it, to put a red pen-mark through the debt and to write by the side of it, "Forgiven; unable to pay."
>
> That man died. After his death his wife looked through his books, and she came upon these marks. She said, "My husband has forgiven people a lot of money. I could use that money very well now." Then she took it to the county court and sued every one of the debtors for the money.
>
> The judge said to her, "How do you know the money is owed?"
>
> "I have it in my husband's books," she replied, and showed him the books.
>
> "Oh, yes. Is this your husband's handwriting?" he asked. "Yes."
>
> "Then," he said, "no court in the world will give you a verdict against people who your husband with his own pen has written 'Forgiven; unable to pay.'"[7]

Jesus Christ carries on intercession for us in heaven;
the Holy Ghost carries on intercession in us on earth;
and we the saints have to carry on intercession for all men.
—OSWALD CHAMBERS

Chapter 4

Jesus Christ, the Attorney of Record

*The Supreme Court of the United States
is the highest court in our land. The only place one
can appeal a Supreme Court decision is in the court of
heaven through prayer.*
—EDDIE SMITH

DEWEY, *Cheatham & Howe*, or "Do we cheat them, and how?", is an old vaudeville comedic name for an imaginary law office. The persons whose names appear on a law office's masthead are usually the owners of the company. Typically they are the more experienced attorneys who have already made a name for themselves in the courtroom and now spend their time as advisors, consultants and promoters for the firm. They often become *figurehead* partners for their law firms. One such figurehead attorney laughingly told us that he mostly plays golf!

In many law firms, however, the names on the masthead are not the only lawyers in the office. Often a firm has other lawyers who faithfully labor in court every day.

When a lawsuit goes to trial, there is always an attorney of record who is personally in charge. Each case must be handled properly if it is to achieve the hoped-for conclusion. The attorney of record, or lead attorney, is ultimately responsible for the strategy (how the case will be presented) and is blamed or rewarded depending on the outcome of the trial.

No matter how many paralegals and associate attorneys work on the case, it is the attorney of record whose license and reputation are on the line. He or she is the one who will ultimately win or lose the case.

"IF THE GLOVE DOESN'T FIT, YOU MUST ACQUIT!"

The attorney of record will often have a team of attorneys to assist him or her. We saw this in the infamous O. J. Simpson case where Johnnie Cochran was the lead attorney. A "dream team" of renowned legal specialists assisted him in the fields of genetics, law enforcement and evidence gathering. Each lawyer on Mr. Cochran's defense team, regardless of age, reputation or experience, was subject to him. It was Johnnie Cochran who set the goals, developed the strategies and determined each attorney's participation.

In her book *A Slow and Certain Light,* Elisabeth Elliot tells of two adventurers who stopped by to see her, all loaded with equipment for the rain forest east of the Andes. They sought no advice, just a few phrases to converse with the Indians.

She writes: "Sometimes we come to God as the two adventurers came to me—confident and, we think, well-informed and well-equipped. But has it occurred to us that with all our accumulation of stuff, something is missing?"

She suggests that we often ask God for too little. "We know what we need—a yes or no answer, please, to a simple question. Or, perhaps a road sign...something quick and easy to point the way.

"What we really ought to have is the Guide Himself. Maps, road signs, a few useful phrases are good things, but infinitely better is someone who has been there before and knows the way."[1] Jesus Christ knows the way. He is our lead attorney, and we are His associates.

THE LEAD ATTORNEY

When we intercede in prayer for something or someone, we petition heaven's court. Depending on the case, we may function as a prosecutor against the forces of darkness, or we may serve on a defense team, pleading mercy for the defendant. In every case, Jesus Christ is our lead attorney. He is the attorney of record.

- *Jesus is responsible for the strategy.* "The Spirit helps us in our weakness. We do not know what we ought to pray for" (Rom. 8:26). The Holy Spirit establishes our prayer assignments.

- *Jesus is ultimately responsible for the success of the case.* "Because Jesus lives forever, he has a permanent priesthood. Therefore he is able to save completely those who come to God through him, because he always lives to intercede for them" (Heb. 7:24–25).

- *Jesus alone is to receive glory for the outcome.* "So whether you eat or drink or whatever you do, do it all for the glory of God" (1 Cor. 10:31). We give God glory for all the victories won through prayer.

- *Only Jesus is to order us to move into warfare prayer against the powers of darkness.* That is another reason we should receive our prayer assignments from Him!

OUR POWER OF ATTORNEY

Jesus said, "And I will do whatever you ask in my name, so that the Son may bring glory to the Father. You may ask me for anything in my name, and I will do it" (John 14:13–14).

In this verse we see that every believer has been given power of attorney. What is power of attorney? *Power of attorney* is simply the legal right to act on someone else's behalf. In our case, we have been granted permission to act in Jesus' name, or on His behalf. The *Encyclopedia Britannica* describes power of attorney as "a written authority, empowering the person named therein to do some act or acts on behalf of the principal, which otherwise could only be done by the principal himself...A power of attorney expires with the death of the principal."[2] Our principal (Christ) is not dead. He's alive! Therefore our power of attorney remains intact.

When I (Alice) was a real estate agent in Northwest Houston, I would frequently direct husbands who traveled overseas in business to sign a power of attorney to enable their wives to sign the legal papers for the purchase of a home. A signed power of attorney was proof to all parties involved of the wife's authority to act on behalf of her husband. In the same way Jesus, before

Jesus Christ, the Attorney of Record

He ascended into heaven, gave His bride power of attorney to act on His behalf! However, this is a serious responsibility, and we should always exercise a prayerful, submissive heart attitude.

David Bryant said, "Here is where praying 'in Jesus' name' finds its true meaning. This is not a phrase to be tacked on to a prayer to indicate that our prayer is finished. Jesus meant for us to pray with authority that comes from our linking our desires with His desires. In essence, we're saying, 'Father, Your Son's life perspective, life direction and life mission are mine, too. They shape everything I am asking You to do.'"[3]

As intercessors we are to pray on Christ's behalf. A wife with power of attorney would misuse that legal right should she decide to purchase a home other than the one she and her husband agreed to purchase. As attorneys in heaven's court, our power of attorney authorizes us to:

- Plead for mercy as a defense attorney on behalf of others—"Brothers, pray for us" (1 Thess. 5:25).

- Act as a prosecuting attorney to expose and defeat the devil according to the intercessory tasks Jesus assigns to us—"The reason the Son of God appeared was to destroy the devil's work" (1 John 3:8). "As the Father has sent me, I [Jesus] am sending you" (John 20:21).

You say, "Great! My mother always hoped I'd become a doctor or a lawyer!" Isn't it amazing that God has called us to partner with Him like this in prayer? When we pray for others, we are actually Jesus' ambassadors using His superior name, under His license (bought with His own blood), with His reputation behind us! Best yet, along with the authority of His name, we are given His credentials of righteousness (2 Cor. 5:21), divine sonship (John 1:12) and joint-heirship (Rom. 8:17) to further guarantee our success!

GOD'S ASSIGNMENTS

Jesus gives us power of attorney and the right to act as associate attorneys only in the cases He authorizes! When God assigns us a case to defend, we must learn to hear His voice and follow His lead. Ezekiel was given an intercessory assignment in Ezekiel 11:1–13:

> Then the Spirit lifted me up and brought me to the gate of the house of the LORD that faces east. There at the entrance to the gate were twenty-five men, and I saw among them Jaazaniah son of Azzur and Pelatiah son of Benaiah, leaders of the people. The LORD said to me, "Son of man, these are the men who are plotting evil and giving wicked advice in this city. They say, 'Will it not soon be time to build houses? This city is a cooking pot, and we are the meat.' Therefore prophesy against them; prophesy, son of man."
>
> Then the Spirit of the LORD came upon me, and he told me to say: "This is what the LORD says: That is what you are saying, O house of Israel, but I know what is going through your mind. You have killed many people in this city and filled its streets with the dead.
>
> "Therefore this is what the Sovereign LORD says: The bodies you have thrown there are the meat and this city is the pot, but I will drive you out of it. You fear the sword, and the sword is what I will bring against you, declares the Sovereign Lord. I will drive you out of the city and hand you over to foreigners and inflict punishment on you. You will fall by the sword, and I will execute judgment on you at the borders of Israel. Then you will know that I am the LORD. This city will not be a pot for you, nor will you be the meat in it; I will execute judgment on you at the borders of Israel. And you will know that I am the LORD, for you have not followed my decrees or kept my laws but

have conformed to the standards of the nations around you."

Now as I was prophesying, Pelatiah son of Benaiah died. Then I fell facedown and cried out in a loud voice, "Ah, Sovereign LORD! Will you completely destroy the remnant of Israel?"

We need to understand the story before we can see the assignment Ezekiel was given. Ezekiel was exiled from Jerusalem into Babylon with the second group of Israelites. God gave him a vision and transported him into Jerusalem where a unique problem was taking place. The prophet saw twenty-five prominent Jerusalem city counselors discussing official policies. In the vision God told Ezekiel that these were the men who were giving wicked counsel to the people of Jerusalem. The men told the people that it was time to rebuild Jerusalem because the city was the cauldron (cooking pot) and they were the meat. As a cauldron protected its contents from the flame, so Jerusalem would protect the people from the Babylonian attack. These men felt they had not been exiled to Babylon because they were favored by God. Their pride was evident in their boasting.

Ezekiel denounced the falsehoods of these twenty-five counselors and told them that Jerusalem would not save them. Some would die by the sword, and others would be dragged away to Babylon. As the prophet was giving the word of the Lord, Pelatiah, the son of Benaiah, suddenly died. *Pelatiah* means "Yahweh's Remnant." Out of Ezekiel's grief that God might destroy all of the remnant of Israel, he fell facedown and cried out, "Ah, Sovereign Lord! Are you going to destroy the entire remnant of Israel in this outpouring of your wrath on Jerusalem?" From this advocacy for the people of Israel, the Lord promised Ezekiel that Israel would return to their homeland and that He would put a new spirit in their hearts. (See Ezekiel 11:17–25.)

The Advocates

Ezekiel was a man who listened to the Father. The assignments that are given to us can be difficult. The courtroom is an adversarial place, a place of confrontation. If you are one who shrinks from confrontation, you should pray that God would grace you with the faith to stand. As the apostle Paul taught in Ephesians 6:13, "Therefore put on the full armor of God, so that when the day of evil comes, you may be able to stand your ground, and after you have done everything, to stand."

And remember that we are not praying *for* Christ, but *with* Him. We serve on His legal team as associate attorneys when we plead our cases in prayer.

In prayer it is better to have a heart without words
than words without a heart.
—JOHN BUNYAN

Chapter 5

Satan, Our
Adversary in Court

*The one concern of the devil is to keep Christians from
praying. He fears nothing from prayerless studies, prayerless
work and prayerless religion. He laughs at our toil, mocks at
our wisdom, but trembles when we pray.*

—SAMUEL CHADWICK

THE devil never takes a holiday—and neither should we. Charles Swindoll relates the following in his book *The Tale of the Tardy Oxcart:*

> The devil takes no holiday; he never rests. If beaten, he rises again. If he cannot enter in front, he steals in the rear. If he cannot enter at the rear, he breaks through the roof or enters by tunneling under the threshold. He labors until he is in. He uses great cunning and many a plan. When one miscarries, he has another at hand and continues his attempts until he wins.[1]

Effective intercession in the court of heaven requires that we provide the best defense for the defenseless. A successful attorney must be able to think like his adversary! We must have enough foresight to expect which arguments our adversary is likely to present during trial. Or, as one attorney explained, "We must anticipate as nearly as possible the strategies that our opposition will use to build their case in order to prepare effective arguments that will destroy them!"

It's another way of restating the oldest rule of war: "Know your enemy!" Let's take a closer look at ours.

LIAR, LIAR

If you happened to see the hilarious Jim Carrey movie *Liar, Liar,* you may remember that the movie's title was based on Carrey's young son's inability to explain his father's occupation to his kindergarten teacher. The movie begins in the classroom with the children being asked to explain what their fathers do for a living. When the teacher asked Carrey's son about his father, the boy explained, "My father is a liar." What he was trying to say was, "My father is a lawyer."

Well, there are a lot of lawyer jokes, but we are not going there. Why? Because there are just as many preacher jokes! And what goes around comes around. Thank You, Lord, for godly Christian attorneys (both men and women) who represent us with integrity.

Every lawyer takes an oath to speak the truth. An *oath* is calling on God as your witness to verify the truth of your words. To lie is to commit perjury. *Perjury* is the voluntary violation of an oath or vow either by swearing to what is untrue or by failing to do what has been promised under oath. Liar, liar...? Did it ever occur to you that lying is actually a language?

THE LANGUAGE OF LIES

Let's take an imaginary journey back in time to the Garden of Eden. Here we find the prosecutor, Satan, and his first attempt at leading a witness into error. We are about to hear his cross-examination of earth's first woman, the mother of mankind, Eve.

In this breathtakingly beautiful, lush, green courtroom, Satan the adversary steps up to the bar of God. "Your Honor," he says, "at this time I would like to call Mrs. Eve to take the stand."

The Judge nods affirmatively, and Eve cautiously moves into the witness stand. An angelic bailiff asks, "Do you swear to tell the truth, the whole truth and nothing but the truth, so help you God?"

Haltingly Eve says, "Yes, I do."

"Be seated," the angel then says to her.

Satan strolls smugly over to the innocent young wife, stops directly in front of her and stares with a cold sarcastic smile. Eve is puzzled. She has no reason to be suspicious or fearful. Yet her stomach tightens, and her heart begins to beat faster. For the first time in this exquisite place, Eve is beginning to feel uncomfortable. After all, she has had no previous interaction with this prosecutor, later to become known as "the accuser of the brethren." Intimidation, one of Satan's favorite tactics, is certainly working on Eve.

Eve is familiar with Adam's handsome face, for he is with her every day. She has even seen her own lovely face in the reflection of Eden's water pools. But this face is different—very different. His is a serpentine face. Having no knowledge of evil, Eve has no category for it. But his peculiar, sinister look troubles her. "Now the serpent was more crafty than any of the wild animals the LORD God had made. He said to the woman, 'Did God really say, "You must not eat from any tree in the garden"?'" (Gen. 3:1).

Innocently Eve attempts to explain, "Oh, no sir. That's not what the Lord said to us at all. He told us that we might eat any fruit in the garden, except the fruit from *that* tree (she points with her finger), the one there in the middle. Sir, God loves us so much that He warned us not to touch it for we would die."

Satan slowly looks up and to the left as he snidely ponders what to say next. Massaging his pointed chin, he smiles wickedly and continues matter-of-factly, "You will *not* die." And in those four words we find the first "not" in the devil's "tale" (pun intended). In fact, Satan has just created an entirely new language on Planet Earth. *It's the language of lies.* And with the first four-word phrase spoken in this new language of lies, Satan accuses his own Maker, the Eternal Judge of the Universe, Judge Jehovah of lying!

The evil one continues, "You see, Mrs. Eve, God knows that as soon as you eat of the fruit of that tree, you will be like Him! You will then know both good *and* evil." Satan was implying that God was trying to keep something good from Eve. Reader, beware! He will try to convince you of the same.

What Satan said *wasn't* entirely a lie. In fact, as a result of Eve and her husband, Adam, eating the forbidden fruit, God said, "The man has now become like one of us, knowing good and evil" (Gen. 3:22).

Satan, the father of lies, is crafty. He knows that if he tells only lies, nobody will believe a word he says. He has found that lies are most effective when they are mixed with truth. That, friend, is the core of every cult.

Lying in court, however, is this prosecutor's favorite tactic. Of this deceiver, Jesus said to the Pharisees in John 8:44, "You belong to your father, the devil, and you want to carry out your father's desire. He was a murderer from the beginning, not holding to the truth, for there is no truth in him. When he lies, he speaks his native language, for he is a liar and the father of lies." Speaks his native language? Yes. Lying *is* a language.

The day that Jesus revealed His impending crucifixion to His disciples, Peter rebuked Him saying, "Never, Lord! This shall never happen to You!" Jesus then turned to Peter and said, "Get behind me, Satan! You are a stumbling block to me" (Matt. 16:21–23). Jesus knew that language! He attributed the statement to Satan, the accuser—the old liar!

Although Jesus never spoke the language of lies, He could interpret it. The trouble with us is that we can, and too often do, speak the language of lies. But far too few of us have the ability to interpret the language! Spiritual naïveté and a lack of spiritual discernment are destroying the integrity and witness of the church today.

Have you ever had an experience that completely changed the way you viewed life? Peter did. Peter was so jolted by Jesus' rebuke that he never forgot the sound of the language of lies he had heard come from his own mouth. The shock and shame of it were indelibly imprinted on his heart.

PETER HEARS THE LANGUAGE OF LIES

Sometime after his own regrettable use of the language of lies, we find Pastor Peter wrestling with a church problem. (See Acts 5.) Ananias had sold a field that belonged to him and had brought the money from the sale and laid it at the apostles' feet.

Perhaps out of jealousy, Ananias, along with his wife, Sapphira, led everyone to believe that the entire profit from the sale of the property was given to the church. In reality, they had kept back some of the money for themselves.

"Ananias," Peter asked, "why did you allow Satan to fill your heart to lie to the Holy Spirit and to keep back part of the proceeds of the land? After all, the land was yours. You have not only lied to us, you have lied to God!"

As soon as Ananias heard Peter's words, he dropped dead on the spot! Three hours later his wife walked in, not knowing what had happened. Peter said to her, "Sapphira, explain to me this land deal that you and Ananias have made."

When she lied to Peter as her husband had, Peter rebuked her saying, "You too have put the Spirit of the Lord to the test. Those who have buried your husband are about to bury you." Immediately she also fell down dead at Peter's feet. (Paraphrased from Acts 5:1–11.)

When Peter heard Ananias and Sapphira lie about their offering to God, he was furious. He immediately recognized the language of lies. Peter said to Ananias, "How is it that Satan has so filled your heart that you have lied to the Holy Spirit?" (Acts 5:3).

The antidote for the lies of our enemy is a thorough knowledge of Scripture. He seeks to steal the witness of the truth from our lips. Even when we have received the truth in our prayer closet, the first goal of the ancient prevaricator is to whisper to us, "God hath not said." Intercessor, we must learn to recognize and interpret the language of lies. How? We counter his courtroom lies with the truth. God's Word is truth!

ACCUSATION

Another of Satan's courtroom tactics is accusation. He is not only the "father of lies," but also "the accuser of the brethren" (Rev. 12:10). Satan wants to kill the purposes of God in our hearts. When we leave the prayer closet and Satan begins to question the ground on which we are standing, he will accuse us before God as he did Job. He accuses us before others as he accused Job before his friends, and he will seek to draw us into self-accusation.

Distinguishing between Satan's voice, the voice of God and our own mental voice isn't always easy. It takes spiritual discernment to know if Satan is lying to us about a truth we have received, or if God is correcting us about a lie we have believed. It can go either way. That's why we must know the Word of God and be submitted to godly counsel. Lack of discernment has caused many intercessors to lose their credibility with church leaders. Intercessors who lose their credibility with leadership often lose the privilege of partnership. We have written a book on this partnership of intercessors and pastors titled *Intercessors and Pastors: The Emerging Partnership of Watchmen and Gatekeepers.* We strongly suggest you read it.

DECEPTION

Satan is not only a liar and an accuser, but he is also a deceiver. As he deceived Eve in the garden, he will also attempt to deceive us, and we are all susceptible to deception. The protection we have against deception is found in knowing the Scripture. It is also found in the ministry of the Holy Spirit who lives within each believer. Jesus promised us this: "But when he, the Spirit of truth, comes, he will guide you into all truth" (John 16:13).

TEMPTATION

Our adversary is shameless. He constantly assaults our minds. He knows that "for as he [a man] thinketh in his heart, so is he" (Prov. 23:7, KJV). So he attacks our minds. We need to take heed to Paul's concern: "But I am afraid that just as Eve was deceived by the serpent's cunning, your minds may somehow be led astray from your sincere and pure devotion to Christ" (2 Cor. 11:3).

Our minds are a battlefield on which we will continually confront him. Our safeguard is to "let this mind be in you, which was also in Christ Jesus" (Phil. 2:5, KJV). A key is for us to "set [our] minds on things above, not on earthly things" (Col. 3:2). The devil's goal has always been, and continues to be, to steal, kill and destroy (John 10:10). He passionately works overtime doing so.

One lawyer told us, "The average professional criminal knows more about criminal law than the average general practice lawyer." Wow! So if unruly and rebellious men know the natural laws of our land, how much more should we be informed of the spiritual laws of God? We who intercede must know the Scriptures if we are to be effective in spiritual warfare. Believe it! Satan and his demons know what God has said.

THE ARMOR OF GOD

We need to know Satan's tactics if we are to successfully plead cases in heaven's court. Paul wrote, "For we are not unaware of his schemes" (2 Cor. 2:11). We are advised to "put on the full armor of God so that you can take your stand against the devil's schemes" (Eph. 6:11).

Let's take a closer look at the armor of God as seen in Ephesians 6:14–17:

The belt of truth

> Stand firm then, with the belt of truth buckled around your waist...

Our knowledge of the Scriptures and our intimate relationship with the Holy Spirit guide us into truth. (See John 17:17.)

The breastplate of righteousness

> ...with the breastplate of righteousness in place...

The righteousness of Christ is what God applies to our lives when He saves us. (See 2 Corinthians 5:21.)

Shoes of peace

> ...with your feet fitted with the readiness that comes from the gospel of peace.

This speaks of our personal preparation and eagerness to share Christ's gospel with those who are lost. (See Romans 1:15.)

The shield of faith

> In addition to all this, take up the shield of faith, with which you can extinguish all the flaming arrows of the evil one.

The shield of faith refers not to our own faith; rather, it is the very faith of Christ Himself, who lives in us. (See Galatians 2:20.)

The helmet of salvation

> Take the helmet of salvation...

The helmet of salvation is our new birth experience and the life of Christ in us. (See Galatians 2:20.)

The sword of the Spirit

> ...and the sword of the Spirit, which is the word of God.

Scripture is the sword of the Spirit. (See Psalm 119:11.)

We do not believe you have to wake up in the morning and quickly "pray on" the armor of God before jumping out of bed.

These truths involve more than invoking a quick prayer. They are lived out in the real world. They involve:

- Experiencing the new birth and the resulting righteousness of Christ
- Being filled with the Holy Spirit
- Meditating on and memorizing God's Word
- Being built up in the furnace of life's afflictions and trials
- Sharing our faith with those who don't know Christ

This—and nothing less—is the armor! As Oswald Chambers wrote, "The armor is for the battle of prayer. The armor is not to fight in, but to shield us while we pray. Prayer is the battle."[2] We must not be ignorant of Satan's devices.

This kind of preparation for trial will equip us to know *the precedent* (what God, the Judge of heaven, has done in the past), *the promises* (the law of God) and *the purposes* of God (His ultimate intention for His creation). As we stand firmly on God's precedent, promises and purposes, we will be able faithfully to plead each case assigned to us, submitting to the supervision of Jesus Christ, our lead attorney, as we trust Him for the outcome!

WHY SATAN SO OFTEN WINS

Dr. Jimmy Draper, president of Lifeway Christian Resources, tells a story of a conversation he had with his saintly mother. Offering a compliment to his mother, Jimmy said, "Mom, I've never heard you criticize anyone. Why, I don't believe you'd speak a critical word against the devil himself."

His mother thought for a moment, then answered, "Well Jimmy, the devil does stick to his job." How true!

For thousands of years, Satan has stuck to his job: to steal, to murder and to destroy. He has found that his methods are especially effective at keeping men from their Creator and hindering the Creator's own children from knowing Him fully! Read the following perfect description of Satan's goal! "The ruthless...the mockers...who have an eye for evil...those who with a word make a man out to be guilty, who ensnare the defender in court and with false testimony deprive the innocent of justice" (Isa. 29:20–21).

As Mrs. Draper said, "Satan sticks to his job." The question we must answer is, "Will we stick to ours?"

JOHN BLANCHARD

John Blanchard stood in Grand Central Station under the big clock. The clock said five minutes until 7:00 P.M., and his heart was racing. At 7:00 P.M. he was to meet a girl he really loved, but he had never ever seen her.

It was during World War II, and John Blanchard was stationed in Florida. One day while reading a book at the base library, he read the marginal notes someone had left behind. He thought to himself, *Wow! What a wonderful person this must be. There's such insight and tenderness here, I would love to know her.* He opened the front of the book, and there was her name, Hollis Maynell. With time and effort he found her address in New York City and wrote her a letter of introduction. The day after he wrote the letter he was shipped to Europe for a tour of duty. Hollis answered John, and they began to communicate with one another.

He soon felt he could share his heart with Hollis, so he told her how scared he was during battles. She counseled him, "Yea, though I walk through the valley of the shadow of death *I will fear no evil,* for thou art with me..." Once he wrote and asked for her picture. She wrote him back, "No deal. Relationships are not built on looks!"

When he completed his tour of duty, he wrote Hollis and

asked if he could meet her and take her to dinner. She agreed and suggested they meet at 7:00 P.M. in Grand Central Station on a certain date. She told him, "You'll recognize me by the red rose I'll be wearing on my lapel." This is his account of that meeting.

A young woman was coming toward me, her figure long and slim. Her blonde hair lay back in curls from her delicate ears; her eyes were blue as flowers. Her lips and chin had a gentle firmness, and in her pale green suit she was like springtime come alive. I started toward her, entirely forgetting to notice she was not wearing a rose.

As I moved, a small, provocative smile curved her lips. "Going my way, sailor?" she murmured. Almost uncontrollably I made one step closer to her, and then I saw Hollis Maynell. She was standing almost directly behind the girl. A woman well past forty, she had graying hair tucked under a worn hat. She was more than plump, her thick-ankled feet thrust into low-heeled shoes.

The girl in the green suit was walking quickly away. I felt as though I was split in two, so keen was my desire to follow her, and yet so deep was my longing for the woman whose spirit had truly companioned me and upheld my own. And there she stood. Her pale, plump face was gentle and sensible, her gray eyes had a warm and kindly twinkle. I did not hesitate. My fingers gripped the small worn blue leather copy of the book that was to identify me to her…

I squared my shoulders and saluted and held out the book to the woman, even though while I spoke I felt choked by the bitterness of my disappointment. "I'm Lieutenant John Blanchard, and you must be Miss Maynell. I am so glad you could meet me; may I take you to dinner?"

The woman's face broadened into a tolerant smile. "I don't know what this is about, son," she answered, "but the young lady in the green suit who just went by, she begged me to wear this rose on my coat. And she said if you were to ask me out to dinner, I should go and tell you that she is waiting for you in the big restaurant across the street. She said it was some kind of test."[3]

Today God is pointing out to us people who are "wearing red roses." These are troubled people who need an advocate to plead their case in heaven's court. Jesus is looking for intercessors who will partner in prayer with Him. The question we must answer is, Will we be distracted by the attractive things the world offers us, or will we remain committed to our kingdom task? Had John Blanchard failed to honor his commitment, he would have missed meeting the love of his life. God is testing us today. We are to pray for the ungodly and stand in the gap for the unattractive issues of life. If we can't pass this test, we will never see our nation revived. Don't forget, Satan will stick to *his* job! So *must* we!

You will find in your "closet of prayer"
what you frequently lose when you are out in the world.
The more you visit it, the more you will want to return.
If you are faithful to your secret place, it will become your
closest friend and bring you much comfort.
The tears shed there bring cleansing.
—Thomas à Kempis

Chapter 6

Here Comes the Judge!

*When our requests are such as honor God,
we may ask as largely as we will. The more daring
the request, the more glory accrues to God when
the answer comes.*

—A. W. Tozer

The Advocates

IT was comedian Flip Wilson who coined the term "Here come 'da Judge!" As we all know, the judge is the central figure in any courtroom. Everything hangs in the balance awaiting his or her decision. An effective attorney knows the judge and knows how the judge tends to rule. Effective spiritual attorneys who plead their cases in court must also know the Judge and how He tends to rule.

Throughout history God has allowed very few of His servants actually to see the Judge's throne. They include Micaiah (1 Kings 22:19), the psalmist David (Ps. 47:8) and the prophet Isaiah (Isa. 6:1).

However, in the fourth chapter of the Book of Revelation, the apostle John records his amazing tour of heaven's courtroom while exiled on the island of Patmos. Jesus appeared to John, showed him an open door to heaven and invited him to enter. John wrote, "At once I was in the Spirit, and there before me was a throne in heaven with someone sitting on it" (Rev. 4:2).

Isn't it interesting that John didn't notice the angels, the streets of gold or the heavenly choir first? The first thing that caught his attention was the throne of the Almighty. That first view of the throne was so overwhelming to John and so central to the message of his book that seventeen of the twenty-two chapters of the Book of Revelation refer to the throne. Who was seated on the throne at the center of heaven's courtroom? It was none other than Judge Jehovah, the Eternal Judge of the Universe (Ps. 93:2).

Thousands of years earlier David had recorded, "The heavens proclaim his righteousness, for God himself is judge" (Ps. 50:6). In the Hebrew language this one intriguing verse gives three descriptions of God: *El, Elohim* and *Jehovah*. These three impressive names present to us three major characteristics of God.

- *El*—the God of Might. *El* means "one God." He is the

Mighty One, the All-powerful One, the One of authority and strength.

- *Elohim*—God of Majesty. *Elohim* is plural. He is one God who exists in three persons. He is the Creator God, the God of greatness, the Supreme God who is sovereign over all.

If these two awesome names of God were our only revelation of Him, He would be unapproachable to us, for they present Him only in His *transcendence*. But He describes Himself in this same verse by another name. This name presents His *immanence*.

- *Jehovah*—the Lord. He is God our Redeemer, the God of mercy who sent His Son to die for us that we might live in covenant fellowship with Him forever! He graciously responds with full understanding to His people.

But our desire is to *see* Jehovah and look upon His face. What does He look like, John?

John continues to describe the Judge he sees seated on heaven's throne as one who has the appearance of jasper and carnelian. What? Jasper and carnelian are precious stones. Jasper is a diamond,[1] and carnelian is a beautiful blood-red stone. One would think these precious stones might describe the inanimate throne on which He sits. No, John is describing God in terms of these colorful stones—or rather the vivid light that radiates from them. In fact, John wrote in another book, "God is light; in him there is no darkness at all" (1 John 1:5). Paul describes God as living in an unapproachable light (1 Tim. 6:16). The psalmist wrote that God is clothed in a garment of light (Ps. 104:2).

Then we remember another passage John wrote. "No one has ever seen God" (John 1:18). In fact, God told Moses, a man who spoke with him face to face (figuratively speaking), "You cannot see my face, for no one may see me and live" (Exod. 33:20).

In the Book of Revelation, John also describes a glistening emerald-green rainbow encircling the throne. We might say that the sparkling *white light* emanating from the diamond represents *God's holiness*, the fiery *red light* of the carnelian stone represents *the shed blood of Jesus,* and the emerald *green rainbow* represents His *mercy.* Since Noah's day, the rainbow has been the promise of salvation. God blends His holiness with His blood and His mercy and reveals Himself as transcendent God, our *immanent* Redeemer!

John is startled to see flashes of lightening and to hear rumblings and peals of thunder coming from the throne. God is not waiting to rule. He is ruling right now. As He listens to the prayers of His people, He continuously decrees and implements His purposes from this throne. The throne of God literally vibrates with divine activity. Interestingly, this is the very phenomenon that Moses and the children of Israel experienced at Mount Sinai, the place where God gave the original Law to Moses (Exod. 19:16–20). But Sinai's fireworks were small compared to this nuclear blast!

To be sure, the Book of Revelation is not casual reading. However, if you are familiar with the Book of Revelation, you know that its themes include awful human suffering, including plagues, tribulation and even martyrdom. It is no mere accident that God reveals His throne before He reveals our future, for heaven's throne is the place of His ultimate rule! There is a certain comfort in knowing that no matter what tomorrow holds for us, God our Redeemer rules in the kingdom of men (Dan. 4:17). He is the Judge to whom we make our intercessory appeals as advocates on behalf of others.

The psalmist David announced:

Here Comes the Judge!

Out of Zion, the perfection of beauty,
    God shines forth.
Our God comes, he does not keep silence,
    before him is a devouring fire,
    round about him a mighty tempest.
He calls to the heavens above
    and to the earth, that he may judge his people:
"Gather to me my faithful ones,
    who made a covenant with me by sacrifice!"
The heavens declare his righteousness
    For God himself is judge!

                    —PSALM 50:2–6, RSV

Our God is *unique.* Nothing and no one compares to Him. Anything said about Him must be based entirely upon His revelation of Himself to us. The reality of His person is greater than any human mind can understand or express. But what do we know of this Judge?

Well, we know that He is omniscient (all-knowing), omnipresent (ever-present) and omnipotent (all-powerful). He has no equal.

Most of us are familiar with Paul's explanation of the fruit of the Spirit. He wrote, "But the fruit of the Spirit is love, joy, peace, patience, kindness, goodness, faithfulness, gentleness and self-control. Against such things there is no law" (Gal. 5:22). The usual application of this passage is that these characteristics are evident in our lives when we are filled with the Spirit. In fact, Paul explains the very process God is performing in us. "For those God foreknew he also predestined to be conformed to the likeness of his Son, that he might be the firstborn among many brothers" (Rom. 8:29). In God's desire to conform us to His likeness, He encourages us to be filled with the Spirit so the Spirit's fruit can be produced in our lives. We are created after His image. But did you ever stop to think that the fruit of the Spirit—since He is God—describes the Judge as well? Read on to see this description.

THE FRUIT OF THE SPIRIT: A PORTRAIT OF OUR GOD

Heaven's Judge is loving.

> He has taken me to the banquet hall, and his banner over me is love.
>
> —SONG OF SOLOMON 2:4

In his book *Written in Blood,* Robert Coleman tells the story of a little boy whose sister needed a blood transfusion. The doctor had explained that she had the same disease the boy had recovered from two years earlier. Her only chance for recovery was a transfusion from someone who had previously conquered the disease. Since the two children had the same rare blood type, the boy was the ideal donor.

"Would you give your blood to Mary?" the doctor asked.

Johnny hesitated. His lower lip started to tremble. Then he smiled and said, "Sure, for my sister."

Soon the two children were wheeled into the hospital room—Mary, pale and thin; Johnny, robust and healthy. Neither spoke, but when their eyes met, Johnny grinned.

As the nurse inserted the needle into his arm, Johnny's smile faded. He watched the blood flow through the tube. With the ordeal almost over, his voice, slightly shaky, broke the silence. "Doctor, when do I die?"

Only then did the doctor realize why Johnny had hesitated, why his lip had trembled when he had agreed to donate his blood. He had thought giving his blood to his sister meant giving up his life. In that brief moment, he had made his great decision.[2]

Fortunately, Johnny didn't have to die to save his sister. But we have a Savior who loved us so much that He did give His life to save us. That is why Paul freely told us, "And I pray that you, being rooted and established in love, may have power, together with all the saints, to grasp how wide and long and high and deep is the love of Christ, and to know this love that surpasses knowledge—that you may be filled to the measure of all the fullness of God" (Eph. 3:17–19).

When we pray, we pray to the Father's heart of love. Perhaps we should take more care to couch our praying in "love words."

Heaven's Judge is joyful.

We serve a joyful God. The prophet Zephaniah wrote, "The LORD your God is with you, he is mighty to save. He will take great delight in you, he will quiet you with his love, he will rejoice over you with singing" (Zeph. 3:17). Our God is not angry with us. The shed blood of Jesus, who became the propitiation for our sins, has satisfied and calmed His outraged holiness. The God who killed sinners in the Old Testament died for them in the New Testament. Paul said it this way:

> But God demonstrates his own love for us in this: While we were still sinners, Christ died for us. Since we have now been justified by his blood, how much more shall we be saved from God's wrath through him! For if, when we were God's enemies, we were reconciled to him through the death of his Son, how much more, having been reconciled, shall we be saved through his life!
> —ROMANS 5:8–10

Like any good daddy, God enjoys His children. He delights in them! He delights in you! Joy should be one of our attributes also. Billy Bray named one of his feet "Glory" and the other "Hallelujah." So whether things went well or not, his feet said, "Glory, Hallelujah! Glory, Hallelujah!"[3]

Knowing that we serve a joyful God should help us frame our

prayers correctly. We are not praying to an angry God. However, we do find Him grieved at times over our sin. Therefore we don't pray *against* people—we pray *for* them in concert with His heart! We don't curse those who curse us, for instance. Jesus taught us a template for life. He said, "But I tell you who hear me: Love your enemies, do good to those who hate you, bless those who curse you, pray for those who mistreat you" (Luke 6:27–28).

- We are to *love* our enemies.
- We are to *do good to* those who use us despitefully.
- We are to *bless* those who curse us.
- And we are to *pray for* (not against) those who persecute us.

Does this template for living that Jesus gave us in Matthew 5:44 describe your petitionary prayers in heaven's court? If our prayers don't line up with Jesus' standards, we shouldn't expect the Judge to decide in our favor. We must align our praying with His character if we expect to win our cases in court.

It is our *spiritual* enemies, Satan and his demonic hosts, that we are to abhor. Paul said that we are to "hate what is evil; cling to what is good" (Rom. 12:9). The prayers that David prayed against his *physical* enemies (men) in the Book of Psalms, we are to pray against our *spiritual* enemies (demonic forces). God's instruction to us is to hate *that* which is evil, not *those* who are evil. We must, as God does, learn to hate sin and love sinners.

It is vitally important that we hate what God hates and love what God loves if we expect Him to render decisions in our favor.

The Judge is peaceful.

Great news! There is no panic in heaven today! God is not nervous! In fact, Isaiah's prophetic announcement concerning the birth of the Messiah (Jesus) says, "His name shall be called Wonderful, Counselor, The mighty God, The everlasting Father, The Prince of Peace" (Isa. 9:6, KJV). The mighty God, the everlasting Father, is also the Prince of Peace! Jesus said of Himself, "Peace I leave with you; my peace I give you. I do not give to you as the world gives. Do not let your hearts be troubled and do not be afraid" (John 14:27).

- When we are born again, we receive *peace with God.*
- When we are being filled with the Holy Spirit, we receive *the peace of God.*
- When we keep our minds focused on the Lord, we are kept in *perfect peace!*

But Isaiah said there is something beyond this. He wrote that God will keep us in *perfect peace* if we keep our minds focused on Him (Isa. 26:3).

Before you plead your case in court, know this: Judge Jehovah is never surprised. Nothing amazes Him. "Oops" is not even in His vocabulary. Unlike earthly judges, He will never be distracted, deceived or manipulated by anyone. We are told in 1 Peter 5:7 to "cast all [our] anxiety on him because he cares for [us]." Boldly petition Him. He is not worried!

Heaven's Judge is patient.

Have you ever complained in your heart to God about folks who seem to get away with sin? We have. It's the old, "If I were God..." syndrome. We are all tempted to don the judge's robe and step behind the bench to render a decision or two at times. Aw, go ahead and admit it; you have, too!

The good thing is, He is God, and we are not. He is the Judge, not us. And with that in mind, perhaps we shouldn't wish judgment on others, lest judgment (not grace) be extended to us. The bottom line is this: All sin will be completely judged. But the omniscient God of heaven will judge it in accordance with His eternal timing!

> But do not forget this one thing, dear friends: With the Lord a day is like a thousand years, and a thousand years are like a day. The Lord is not slow in keeping his promise, as some understand slowness. He is patient with you, not wanting anyone to perish, but everyone to come to repentance.
>
> —2 PETER 3:8–9

Intercessory warriors can easily become impatient. After all, one of the characteristics common to intercessors is that we are seldom satisfied with the status quo. One night I (Eddie) preached that statement, and an intercessor near the front of the auditorium shrieked spontaneously. I stopped and asked, "Are you all right?"

"Oh yes," she replied. "But you have just affirmed me. I've always thought there was something wrong with me, because the whole time I was growing up my family would complain, 'You're just never satisfied, are you?'"

A holy dissatisfaction with the way things are is common to God's intercessors. However, we must not let that carry over in the way we approach Jehovah. We need to yield our burdens to His timetable. Pray confidently with a boldness. Then expect answers.

That's why Hebrews 11:13 challenges each of us who plead our cases in prayer to pray in faith and to leave the results to God. It says, "All these people [Noah, Abraham, Isaac, Jacob and others] were still living by faith when they died. They did not receive the things promised; they only saw them and welcomed them from a distance." They died, having not received that for which they were praying. But they died in faith, believing! If we insist on operating on our own timetable, we may become impatient with God. We want to see revival, and we want to see it *now*—even sooner if possible! But God has His own schedule to keep. The tough question we must answer is this: Will I faithfully plead the prayer cases that God has assigned to me even if I don't live to see the results? This is the true mark of faith.

Don't forget. Our omniscient God knows the end from the beginning. He doesn't meter justice on the scale of time. He meters justice on the scale of eternity. You are praying today to a patient God.

The Judge is kind.

We were watching a political commercial for a judge who was running for reelection. Judge Scott Brister was listening to the tick of a stopwatch in his hand. He looked up and said to the viewing audience, "Every one should have a fair trial in court. I am not short on fairness or justice. But time is of the essence. That's why I will, as your judge, make sure that the cases in my court will be dealt with fairly, quickly and with justice." Aren't we grateful to have a Judge that is not only fair and just, but He is all-knowing as well?

Galatians 2:6 promises, "God does not judge by external appearance."

Peter said in Acts 10:34–35, "I now realize how true it is that God does not show favoritism but accepts men from every nation who fear him and do what is right." Our God is no respecter of persons. There is level ground at the foot of the cross. Our Judge has feelings and is touched with our infirmities. He listens. And He is never "too tired to talk."

My (Alice) mother told me about a time when I was around four years old and came out of my Sunday school class crying. She asked me why I was crying.

"I feel sorry for Jesus," was my tearful response.

"Why do you feel sorry for Jesus?" my mother asked.

"Because Jesus doesn't have any blue jeans. He only has a nightgown to wear," was my dramatic reply. My compassion was immature, but real. But of God's compassion for us, Isaiah 66:13 says, "As a mother comforts her child, so will I comfort you."

King David told God, "You discern my going out and my lying down; you are familiar with all my ways" (Ps. 139:3). Isaiah said of Him, "He was despised and rejected by men, a man of sorrows, and familiar with suffering" (Isa. 53:3). We see this in Paul's description of the ministry of the Holy Spirit: "In the same way, the Spirit helps us in our weakness. We do not know what we ought to pray for, but the Spirit himself intercedes for us with groans that words cannot express" (Rom. 8:26). What a kind and compassionate God we have!

Our heavenly Father longs to express His compassion, yet when the Jews rejected Jesus as their Messiah, from atop Mount Olivet, with great emotion, Jesus wept, "O Jerusalem, Jerusalem, you who kill the prophets and stone those sent to you, how often I have longed to gather your children together, as a hen gathers her chicks under her wings, but you were not willing" (Matt. 23:37).

Let's thank God for His kindness to us.

Heaven's Judge is good.

Around the Judge's head fly four living creatures continuously crying above the thunder and lightening, and above the roar of the praising multitudes, "Holy, holy, holy is the Lord who was, who is and who is to come!"

One day I (Eddie) quipped, "God, I think to have those six-winged creatures flying around my head like gnats, crying twenty-four hours a day, seven days a week, would drive me crazy!"

God gently said, "Eddie, can't you see how unlike Me you are?" Ouch!

God announces, "Be holy, because I am holy" (1 Pet. 1:16). God is a holy Judge. After all, *Holy* is the first name of His Spirit!

He is a righteous Judge who knows our thoughts before we

think them and our words before we speak them. He actually judges us according to the intents of our hearts!

His judgments are righteous and just for two reasons. First, because nothing less can proceed from Him. Second, His judgments are just because His decisions are based on perfect knowledge. Contrast that with the limitations of an earthly judge.

A mother of three young children is pulled over by a patrolman for failing to stop at a stop sign. What happened? She was seriously distracted by one of her small children and failed to see the sign in time to stop. In essence she didn't know there was a sign there at all. God's Word says, "Anyone, then, who knows the good he ought to do and doesn't do it, sins" (James 4:17). She clearly didn't know.

An earthly judge hearing this case would have no choice but to punish the young mother for failing to stop. Why? Because the earthly judge, unlike God, doesn't have all knowledge and can't possibly know the intent of the heart. We are interceding to the heart of a good and holy God who judges accordingly.

Heaven's Judge is faithful.

From the top of Mount Washburn in Yellowstone National Park, a bald eagle gracefully glides on pinions, motionless, two thousand feet above the surface of the earth. He descends. Then he ascends again on the warm currents of air. That eagle would drop like a rock could he not trust his wings. Trust in God is not an indefinite feeling amid vacancy. Trust is a definite grasp upon that which can lift you where you otherwise could not go. But there must be Someone to whom your trust and faith can be attached. That someone is God. We all find comfort in these words: "Even youths grow tired and weary, and young men stumble and fall; but those who hope [trust] in the LORD will renew their strength. They will soar on wings like eagles; they will run and not grow weary, they will walk and not be faint" (Isa. 40:30–31).

There is comfort in realizing that a God who cannot lie has

promised, "I the Lord do not change" (Mal. 3:6). Hebrews 13:8 reminds us that "Jesus Christ is the same yesterday and today and forever."

How true the words of the songwriter, who penned:

> Great is Thy faithfulness, O God my Father,
> There is no shadow of turning with Thee;
> Thou changest not, Thy compassions, they fail not;
> As Thou hast been, Thou forever wilt be.[4]

We are to be expressions of His faithfulness. As we live lives empowered by the Holy Spirit, we will be faithful. And as we plead our cases in prayer, we do so before a faithful Judge!

Heaven's Judge is gentle.

James the Apostle wrote, "Mercy triumphs over judgment!" (James 2:13). What a comforting thought, especially when we stand before Him charged with a crime.

The story is told about an earnest Christian man who became a judge in his local town. One morning there appeared before him in the court a friend of his youth who had strayed and committed an offense against the law of the land. Those who knew the relationship between the two men expected the judge to deal mercifully, but they were very much surprised when he went to the officer of the court and took from his own pocket the money to pay the fine.

He did his duty as a judge and upheld the law, but he showed something of the mercy of God for his friend when he paid the penalty. There is little wonder that the lawbreaker was broken-hearted in his repentance.[5]

If our God is a God of mercy, we should be people of mercy. Jesus taught, "Blessed are the merciful, for they will be shown mercy" (Matt. 5:7). We reap what we sow. Always remember that anything you have received from God was on its way to others when it got to you. Since you are a *recipient* of mercy, become a *distributor!* When you plead in prayer, plead for mercy!

Heaven's Judge exercises self-control.

While watching a television special on the panda bears of China, we were amazed at how tiny their offspring are when they are born. Although they will weigh several hundred pounds when they are full grown, at birth they are mouselike in size. The mother panda held her tiny baby completely inside her mouth!

Imagine the grace with which an omnipotent, indestructible God deals with this fragile planet and the people who live on it. Imagine the self-control our all-powerful God exercises when dealing with the likes of us. It would take one distraction, and the entire earth and everyone on it would vanish in a puff of smoke.

Finally, we should know that the Judge's decisions are sometimes *yes,* sometimes *no* and sometimes *not yet.* Many of His decisions are *if/then* decisions. They are decisions that are contingent upon our responses. A perfect example can be found in the following familiar verse:

> *If* my people, who are called by my name, will humble themselves and pray and seek my face and turn from their wicked ways, *then* will I hear from heaven and will forgive their sin and will heal their land.
> —2 CHRONICLES 7:14, EMPHASIS ADDED

Clearly, if we don't humble ourselves, pray, seek His face and turn from our wickedness, then He won't hear, forgive and heal our land.

The Father has no favorites, but He does have intimates.
—ALICE SMITH

Chapter 7

Personal Preparation

Make prayer a daily, moment-to-moment
adventure in your life.
—Eddie Smith

The Advocates

ANY attorney will assure you that proper preparation is the key to winning a trial decision. Nestor stood before the Greek generals at Troy and said, "The secret of victory is in getting a good ready."[1] As spiritual advocates, it is crucial that we get a "good ready" before we face the battles that lie ahead. When we intercede in prayer, we plead our case before the eternal Judge of the universe. Every case we present to God calls for genuine preparation. Without proper preparation a lawyer would make a fool of himself before the judge, his client, his adversary and the gallery of people!

SELF-EVALUATION

Consider the following four items in relation to your own life.

The new birth

Before we prepare a case, we must first prepare ourselves. Personal preparation to plead a case in intercessory prayer before God's throne begins with the new birth. (See John 3:1–5). Without salvation, we are not prepared to face our own trials or anyone else's! But exactly what is salvation?

Salvation is not adopting a new belief system or code of ethics. It is not a commitment to attend church, and it is far more than mental aerobics.

First Corinthians 2:14 says, "The man without the Spirit does not accept the things that come from the Spirit of God, for they are foolishness to him, and he cannot understand them, because they are spiritually discerned." A person without salvation is a person without the Spirit of Christ. In Romans 8:9 we read, "And if anyone does not have the Spirit of Christ, he does not belong to Christ."

Salvation begins with a revelation of the *absence* of a personal relationship with Jesus Christ and the overwhelming awareness of our personal sin before a perfect God. It is vital that we each settle this in our own hearts. But salvation is more than the forgiveness and removal of our sin. We are empowered to live because the Holy Spirit moves in. A Christian is a person in whom the Holy Spirit lives. We are unprepared to live or to die without the Spirit of Christ alive in our hearts. The mystery of eternal life is, "...Christ in you, the hope of glory" (Col. 1:27).

We asked several lawyers what makes a good attorney. One of them said, "A good attorney is one who knows the judge and knows how he tends to rule." We might add that a good intercessor is one who knows God and knows how He tends to rule!

Faith in God

Through the new birth we can truly *know* God. Being born into His family, we become His children. As children of God who spend time in His Word and in His presence, we begin to know Him as He really is, not as we have supposed Him to be. An attorney who knows the judge and how he tends to rule has a distinct advantage over an attorney who does not. One can have no stronger position in the heavenly court than to be one of the Judge's own children. Who would dare challenge us? Or, as Paul wrote, "If God is for us, who can be against us?" (Rom. 8:31).

Another lawyer answered our question this way. He said, "A good attorney is one the judge knows and finds to be both credible and persuasive."

Speaking of the last judgment, Jesus said, "Many will say to me on that day, 'Lord, Lord, did we not prophesy in your name, and in your name drive out demons and perform many miracles?' Then I will tell them plainly, 'I never knew you. Away from me, you evildoers!'" (Matt. 7:22–23). As important as it is to know God, it is equally important that He know us!

"Doesn't God know everybody?" you might ask. In a creative sense He does. We know several children in our neighborhood, but we know none of them the way we know our own daughter Ashlee. (Ashlee, our youngest daughter, is the only one of our children still at home.) Paul wrote to Timothy, "Nevertheless, God's solid foundation stands firm, sealed with this inscription: 'The Lord knows those who are his...'" (2 Tim. 2:19).

A pastor whom we know told us the story of a family in his church whose young son suffered from a life-threatening disease. His parents, not seeing the results they had hoped for, took their child off the prescribed course of treatment for an alternative therapy. The medical officials called Children's Protective Services and had the parents charged with child endangerment.

A trial date was set, and the family court judge was scheduled to hear the charges. A famed, high-powered Christian attorney volunteered to defend them. The day the trial began, the judge was already seated at the bench reviewing the charges when the family's attorney walked into the courtroom and made his way to his chair. The judge saw him enter, and before their attorney could take his seat, the judge uncharacteristically left the bench, walked over and warmly welcomed him with a bear hug. It so happened that the family's attorney had been the judge's mentor early in his legal career.

Want to bet on which side won the case? You're right! The judge ruled in favor of the parents. The best lawyer to have is not necessarily the most experienced or the most skilled.

There are some important considerations that will determine your effectiveness in pleading cases in heaven's court. These include the following:

- Do you know the Judge? And does He know you? Is He truly your Father? Have you been born again? "Nevertheless, God's solid foundation stands firm, sealed with this inscription: 'The Lord knows those who are his,' and, 'Everyone who confesses the name of the Lord must turn away from wickedness'" (2 Tim. 2:19).

- Do you know how the Judge tends to rule? Do you

know His ways, why He does what He does? "He made known his ways to Moses, his deeds to the people of Israel" (Ps. 103:7).

- Does the Judge find you to be credible and persuasive? "For the eyes of the Lord are on the righteous and his ears are attentive to their prayer, but the face of the Lord is against those who do evil" (1 Pet. 3:12).

- Do you have faith that Judge Jehovah will hear and answer you? "And without faith it is impossible to please God, because anyone who comes to him must believe that he exists and that he rewards those who earnestly seek him" (Heb. 11:6).

Know your position in Christ

In every state an attorney must meet certain requirements, which include a very difficult bar exam. So it is with us who pray. We need to be properly equipped. (See Ephesians 4:11–13.) The courtroom is an adversarial place. It is a place of confrontation and conflict. As our friend Dr. Mickey Bonner used to say, "All prayer is warfare." If we don't know our position in Christ, we may be easily intimidated by the devil. If we are to be effective in intercessory prayer, we must be secure in Christ. If we are to expect to win a case against Satan we must know that Christ is in us!

It is not only important to know what Scripture says about the case we plead, but we must also know what it says about us! Paul writes to the Christians in Colosse, "For in Christ all the fullness of the Deity lives in bodily form, and you have been given fullness in Christ, who is the head over every power and authority" (Col. 2:9–10). The King James Version says, "Ye are complete in him!"

Knowing your position in Christ fortifies you before the bar of God. It also fortifies you before your adversary!

The seven sons of Sceva are a good example of advocates who went out half-cocked and unprepared to face their adversary. They were not personally prepared to go to court!

> Some Jews who went around driving out evil spirits tried to invoke the name of the Lord Jesus over those who were demon-possessed. They would say, "In the name of Jesus, whom Paul preaches, I command you to come out." Seven sons of Sceva, a Jewish chief priest, were doing this. One day the evil spirit answered them, "Jesus I know, and I know about Paul, but who are you?" Then the man who had the evil spirit jumped on them and overpowered them all. He gave them such a beating that they ran out of the house naked and bleeding.
>
> —Acts 19:13–16

These boys had no position in Christ! They were at the mercy of their adversary. While the court shows mercy from time to time, the adversary, as the sons of Sceva learned, shows none!

A pastor asked a church member one Sunday morning, "And how are you doing?"

The member replied, "Oh, pretty good, under the circumstances."

To which the pastor responded, "And just what are you doing *under* your circumstances?"

We are not to live our lives according to our earthly circumstances. We are to live according to our position in Christ! It is written that in Christ we are:

- New creations—2 Corinthians 5:17
- The temple of God—1 Corinthians 3:16
- Able to do all things through Christ—Philippians 4:13
- Perfected forever—Hebrews 10:14

- Seated in the heavenlies—Ephesians 1:3–6
- A chosen generation—1 Peter 2:9
- A royal priesthood—1 Peter 2:9
- God's possession—Ephesians 1:14
- Chosen of God—Ephesians 1:11
- An heir of God—Galatians 4:7
- Predestined to be conformed into Christ's image—Romans 8:29
- A holy nation—1 Peter 2:9
- A people who belong to God—1 Peter 2:9
- Complete in Him—Colossians 2:9–10
- The righteousness of God—2 Corinthians 5:21
- A kingdom of priests—Revelation 1:6

It is extremely difficult for the adversary to intimidate those who know who they are in Christ and who are intimately acquainted with Him!

Developing intimacy with God

Without a doubt, the most difficult part of our Christian life is to understand how we can relate intimately with a God we cannot see. Yet our communion relationship with our heavenly Bridegroom will determine our effectiveness as intercessory attorneys.

We love the story about the elderly man and wife that is written in Alan D. Wright's book *Lover of My Soul.*

An elderly couple sat across the breakfast table on the morning of their fiftieth wedding anniversary. The husband put down the paper and spoke to his wife: "After fifty years of marriage, I've found you tried and true."

Unfortunately the aging wife was hard of hearing. "Eh? What's that you say?"

The man spoke louder. "I said, 'After fifty years of marriage, I've found you tried and true!"

"What?" the wife complained over her squeaking hearing aid.

Nearly shouting, the husband tried again: "AFTER FIFTY YEARS OF MARRIAGE, I'VE FOUND YOU TRIED AND TRUE!"

The old wife lifted her nose and snooted, "Well, after fifty years of marriage, I'm tired of you, too!"[2]

A bride must never tire of her bridegroom. Tragically, the church is the only bride that hardly knows her Bridegroom.

In this relationship of divine love, it is in the heart of Jesus to have a close intimate friendship. Yet the reason intimacy is often overlooked is because love is always tested. And when we try to get close to God and a huge test comes, we back up and sometimes forget the process that is most needful to know the Lord in a deeper way. When the tests come, the silence of God often accompanies them. Remember, the teacher never talks during the test. We must realize that just because the Lord is silent doesn't mean we are faithless or in sin or that God has put us on the shelf. The Father is monitoring our desire for a deeper relationship with Him.

Instead of waiting on God during our wilderness of silence, we try to perform or ignore the silence. We need trials to purify us, but God's argument is that instead of "counting it all joy when you fall into divers (various) kinds of trials," we moan, groan and become unwilling to continue the process. (See James 1:2.) The process determines our qualification for future assignments. Permit us to say it this way: Our gift or anointing won't take us where our character can't keep us! So learn to submit to the tests! It can be a real learning experience if you will let it!

QUALITIES OF A GOOD ADVOCATE

Following are personal and professional qualities that make good attorneys. Let's look to see how these qualities also help make good intercessors.

Personal Preparation

Dedication

An intercessor must be committed to Christ, to others and to the task of intercession. There simply is no substitute for dedication. As Phillips Brooks once said, "If man is man and God is God, to live without prayer is not merely an awful thing; it is an infinitely foolish thing."[3]

Reliability

It's not our *ability* that God looks for, but our *availability.* Paul Daniel Rader once said, "If you can beat the devil in the matter of regular daily prayer, you can beat him anywhere. If he can beat you there, he can possibly beat you anywhere." Or as one country preacher once said, "If your day is hemmed with prayer, it's less likely to come unraveled."

Integrity

In my (Alice) book *Beyond the Veil,* I write:

> If we accept an assignment from God, we can be sure that He will attempt to build integrity into our lives. I love Psalm 26:11–12: "But I lead a blameless life; redeem me and be merciful to me. My feet stand on level ground; in the great assembly I will praise the LORD."
>
> My paraphrase would read: "In all my public trust I will walk uprightly and pay strict attention to truth, honesty, justice and mercy. I will not plan evil schemes or use myself to promote my own cause. I will be true to the integrity of the Word. I will live a moral life in private and in public. I stand firmly on principles of proper conduct and I will not turn aside."[4]

Objectivity and empathy

Objectivity and empathy are tricky. Both are necessary, but they must be kept in balance.

If we are empathetic intercessors who cannot find objectivity in prayer, we will soon be consumed emotionally and ultimately overwhelmed with the prayer needs we bear. Remember the old song that says, "Take your burden to the Lord and leave it there."[5]

If we are objective intercessors without empathy who cannot feel the needs of those for whom we have been commissioned to pray, our prayer life will grow stale and eventually dry up.

Kind

Kindness is a necessary commodity for the intercessor/advocate, as illustrated by the following story: An old man carried a little can of oil with him everywhere he went. If he passed through a door with squeaky hinges, he put a little oil on the hinges. If the gate was hard to open, he poured a little oil upon the latch. Every day he found a variety of ways to use his pocket oilcan to advantage. Neighbors thought he was eccentric, but he went on his way, doing all within his power to lubricate the hard places and make life easier and more enjoyable for others.[6]

Do we carry with us the oil of human kindness? When the traffic is backed up, the grocery clerk is rude or your boss decides to come down on you, are you exercising the oil of gladness? Go ahead and do it... it will make your day.

Discipline

The intercessor will not be successful without applying discipline to his or her work of intercession. As the visitor to a pottery factory observed, discipline is vitally important:

> A visitor to a famous pottery establishment was puzzled by an operation that seemed aimless. In one room there was a mass of clay beside a workman. Every now and then he took up a large mallet and struck several smart blows on the surface of the lump. Curiosity led to the question: "Why do you do that?"

"Wait a bit, sir, and watch it," was the reply.

The visitor obeyed, and soon the top of the mass began to heave and swell. Bubbles formed upon its face. "Now sir, you will see," said the modeler with a smile. "I could never shape the clay into a vase if these air bubbles were in it, therefore I gradually beat them out."

It sounded in the ears of the visitor like an allegory of Romans 4:3–5, "Tribulation worketh patience ... experience ... hope." Is not the discipline of life, so hard to bear sometimes, just a beating out of the bubbles of pride and self-will, so the Master may form a vessel of earth to hold heavenly treasures?[7]

Leadership ability

In his book *Wind and Fire,* Bruce Larson points out some interesting facts about sandhill cranes:

> These large birds that fly great distances across continents have three remarkable qualities. First, they rotate leadership. No one bird stays out in front all the time. Second, they choose leaders who can handle turbulence. And then, all during the time one bird leads, the rest honk their affirmation. That's not a bad model for the church. Certainly we need leaders who can handle turbulence and who are aware that leadership ought to be shared. But most of all, we need a church where we all honk encouragement.[8]

It is safe to say that some of our prayer assignments are also being borne by other Christians. Let's guard our hearts against feeling that we—and our prayers—are "the only reasons" something happens. As the apostle Paul warned us, "Do not think of yourself more highly than you ought, but rather think of yourself with sober judgment, in accordance with the measure of faith God has given you" (Rom. 12:3).

High moral character

A Buddhist monk in Sri Lanka, who was acquainted with both Christianity and Buddhism, was once asked what he thought was the great difference between the two. He replied, "There is much that is good in each of them, and probably in all religions. But what seems to me to be the greatest difference is that you Christians know what is right and have the power to do it, while we Buddhists know what is right but have not any such power."[9]

The monk was right. True freedom is not *the right* to do as we please. It is *the power* to do what is right!

A story was told by a lawyer who lived in the chambers in the temple of how, in the room next to his, there was an old gray-haired man who knelt down every night and said his prayers aloud. The partition between their rooms was thin, and he heard what the old man said quite distinctly. He was greatly surprised to hear him always say this prayer: "Lord, make me a good boy."

This may seem rather ludicrous. But if you think of it, you will be touched by its beauty. Long years before when, as a little child that old man had knelt at his mother's knee, she had taught him this petition, "Lord, make me a good boy."

And through the years with their trials and temptations, he still felt the need of offering that cry in the old, simple language of childhood, knowing that in the sight of the ageless God he was still a child.[10]

Just as a good advocate should be a person of high moral character, an effective intercessor must also live a holy life of high moral character.

A team player

Corporate intercession is almost an unknown art. In most places it is individual intercession in a corporate setting. Thankfully, the church is beginning to understand how to gather as a group and approach God as one person!

We are also beginning to network as intercessors. We realize that the more testimonies we have in court, the stronger our case will be. We are grateful for the sixty-one personal intercessors who faithfully serve us and our ministry in prayer. We take seriously the hours they spend in court on our behalf.

We never cease to be amazed at the self-discipline exerted by intercessors. The abilities to work well under pressure and with minimal supervision are grace gifts that God has given most intercessors. People of prayer, we admire your faithfulness to voluntarily spend the time you do in prayer on behalf of others.

We can experience transformation of our families, cities and nations if we will be willing to labor together.

The prayer of the feeblest saint on earth who
lives in the Spirit and keeps right with God is a terror to Satan.
The very powers of darkness are paralyzed by prayer;
no spiritual séance can succeed in the presence of a
humble praying saint. No wonder Satan tries to
keep our minds fussy in active work till we
cannot think in prayer.
—OSWALD CHAMBERS

Chapter 8

Case Preparation:
Defending Others in Court

*To clasp the hands in prayer is the beginning of an uprising
against the disorder of the world.*

–K. B.

AN old man walking the beach at dawn noticed a young man ahead of him picking up starfish and flinging them into the sea. Catching up with the youth, he asked what he was doing. The answer was that the stranded starfish would die if left until the morning sun.

"But the beach goes on for miles, and there are millions of starfish," countered the old man. "How can your effort make a difference?"

The young man looked at the starfish in his hand and then threw it to safety in the waves. "It makes a difference to this one," he said.[1]

Every intercessory assignment carried out in the court of heaven, no matter how big or small, makes a difference to someone. However, our effectiveness in prayer will be determined by the way we as defense attorneys plead the case. On July 15, 1866, famous preacher C. H. Spurgeon delivered a splendid message titled "Order and Argument in Prayer." In that message Rev. Spurgeon emphasized three key steps to effective prayer.

1. It is needful that our (case) suit be ordered before God.

Spurgeon said, "The ancient saints were wont, with Job, to order their cause before God; that is to say, as a petitioner coming into Court does not come there without thought to state his case on the spur of the moment, but enters into the audience chamber with his suit well prepared, having moreover learned how he ought to behave himself in the presence of the great One to whom he is appealing. It is well to approach the seat of the King of kings as much as possible with premeditation and preparation, knowing what we are about, where we are standing, and what it is which we desire to obtain."

2. Part of prayer is filling the mouth with arguments.

Case Preparation: Defending Others in Court

"Not to fill the mouth with words, nor good phrases, nor pretty expressions, but filling the mouth with arguments are the knocks of the rapper by which the gate is opened. Why are arguments to be used at all? Is the first enquiry? The reply being, certainly not, because God is slow to give, not because we can change the divine purpose, not because God needeth to be informed of any circumstance with regard to ourselves or of anything in connection with mercy asked: The arguments to be used are for our own benefit, not for His. He requires for us to plead with Him, and to bring forth our strong reasons, as Isaiah saith, because this will show that we feel the value of mercy. When a man searches for arguments for a thing it is because he attaches importance to that which he is seeking. Again our use of arguments teaches us the ground upon which we obtain the blessing. Besides, the use of arguments is intended to stir up our fervency."

3.   If the Holy Ghost shall teach us how to order our case and how to fill our mouth with arguments, the result shall be that we shall have our mouth filled with praises.

"The man who has his mouth full of arguments in prayer shall soon have his mouth full of benedictions in answer to prayer. It is said—I know not how truly—that the explanation of the text, 'Open thy mouth wide and I will fill it,' may be found in a very singular Oriental custom. It is said that not many years ago—I remember the circumstance being reported—the king of Persia ordered the chief of his nobility, who had done something or other which greatly gratified him, to open his mouth, and when he had done so he (the king) began to put into his mouth pearls, diamonds, rubies and emeralds, till he had filled it as full as it could hold, and then he bade him go his way. Now certainly whether that be an explanation of the text or not it is an illustration of it. God says, 'Open thy mouth with arguments,' and then

He will fill it with mercies priceless, and unspeakably valuable. Oh! Let us then open wide our mouth when we have to plead with God. Our needs are great, let our asking be great, and the supply shall be great too."[2]

Now we have been encouraged to argue our case by one of history's greatest orators.

Before we look into Scripture to learn how to order our argument, we need to learn a couple of legal terms. The *defendant* is a person who has to answer the legal action brought against him. The role of the defendant is to plead for the mercy of the court by humbling himself before the Lord. The *defense attorney* is one who represents the defendant by developing a case to present to the Judge. The role of the attorney is to:

- Seek the purposes of God in the issue.
- Uncover the plans of the enemy.
- State the evidence.
- Refer to the law of God.
- Petition heaven for mercy. (See James 2:13.)
- Ask for a definite answer.

OUR MODEL FOR DEFENSE

In Exodus 32:11–14 we find a classic case of courtroom drama as Moses, like a defense attorney, pleads a case brought against the Israelites (the defendants). The principles contained in this case prepared by Moses become our model for our work as defense attorney advocates/intercessors in our world today. Notice the clear legal structure Moses employs in the Israelites' defense. The defense attorney will utilize:

1. *The facts*—the conditions that exist as he sees them.

2. *The evidence*—proof that it is as the facts state.

3. *The law*—what God's Word says regarding this issue.

4. *Court precedent*—what God (the court) has done in the past in similar situations.

5. *The Judge's character*—he will also plead his case based on the Judge's character.

6. *The prayer*—he will clearly and succinctly state the decision he is asking the Judge to make.

7. *The decision*—the decision is the Judge's final conclusion of the matter.

Let's take a thorough look at each of these seven principles as we prepare to become defense attorney advocates/intercessors for those who need our support. These building blocks will provide an additional foundation on which we can build an effective prayer strategy. A good presentation will include several, if not all, of the following:

Collect the facts

If we don't know the facts, we are likely to pray amiss. After all, it is the facts that are on trial! The law doesn't determine whether you will win or lose the case. A clear presentation of the facts is what determines the decision.

A lady came down the aisle during a revival meeting one night to ask me (Eddie) to pray that God would heal her lungs. She was about to have part of one lung surgically removed. As she made her request, I was overpowered by the smell of cigarette smoke on her breath. "Do you smoke cigarettes?" I asked.

"Why yes," she answered reluctantly.

"Do you actually expect me to pray that our heavenly Father will give you new lungs while you willfully destroy the set of lungs you have?" I asked her. To pray for her healing without her willingness to turn from her self-destructive behavior would have been foolish. Thankfully, she did repent and turn from her addiction that night. Her husband came to the altar and forsook his nicotine addiction as well. I also have a good report. When she went to the doctor for the final exam before her operation, she was told that the operation was not necessary after all!

Another lady asked for prayer that she would stop smoking. Suddenly I (Eddie) received a word from the Lord. "Why do you hate your father?" I asked her.

She looked surprised and answered, "I don't hate my father."

"You don't like him," I probed further.

"You're right; I don't like my father," she admitted.

"In fact, you are angry with him," I challenged.

"OK, I'm angry...well yes, I hate my father! But what's that got to do with anything?" she exploded.

When she repented of her hatred and forgave her father, she never desired another cigarette. The cigarettes were only a smoke screen Satan used to keep her blind to the real issue. The important point is that to minister effectively as a counselor or intercessor, we must first ascertain the facts and ask God to disclose any deception before we agree to petition heaven for results.

Spiritual mapping

Spiritual mapping is the act of researching a city's past to learn what historical facts may have empowered the enemy and given him legal rights. It requires research and spiritual discernment to be an effective researcher. To know the facts of a city is critical as we plead the case in prayer. An attorney knows that the smallest detail, if overlooked, can destroy his case. As London lawyer (barrister) John Saunders said in a *People* magazine article, "To be a good lawyer, you really do have to have a sense of history."[3]

Collect the evidence

Collecting evidence is central in the preparation to plead any case. Attorneys have detectives, medical and forensic experts and paralegals to help collect the evidence. The situation, the facts, the circumstances, the witnesses, the possible motives and the credibility of the accused are important issues to take into account. In intercession we must also seek to know the purposes of God and the purposes of Satan, because God's ways are not like our ways (Isa. 55:9). We need to seek His heart for understanding before we move forward. We will increase our victories in court when we receive a burden from God with an undivided and pure heart.

Study the law

Perhaps unanswered prayer has you frustrated. Have you ever sat down and asked yourself what is missing in your prayers? Any number of things may hinder you. However, it may be God's Word that's missing in your prayers.

Lawyers and their paralegal staffs often search and research the law for hundreds of hours. There are lawsuits that have been lost because the lawyers who handled the case did not know about an obscure law written two hundred years before that could have given them the edge. Before Joshua died, he told the children of Israel, "Now I am about to go the way of all the earth. You know with all your heart and soul that not one of all the good promises the LORD your God gave you has failed. Every promise has been fulfilled; not one has failed" (Josh. 23:14).

E. M. Bounds once said:

> Unless the vital forces of prayer are supplied by God's Word, prayer, though earnest, even vociferous in its urgency, is in reality flabby, vapid and void. The absence of vital force in praying can be traced to the absence of a constant supply of God's Word, to repair the waste, and renew the life. He who would learn to pray well, must first study God's Word, and store it in his memory and thought.[4]

In the court of heaven, Scripture is the law! When we approach God with His Word, we can be assured of a heavenly audience. Each argument we make before Judge Jehovah should be offered on the basis of what He has said. After all, the law (Scripture) is the language of the court. So, prayer is an appeal of faith based on the Word of God. Sometimes we can predict the verdict God will render because we know what God has said.

Obviously David knew the law when he prayed, "And now, Lord, let the promise you have made concerning your servant and his house be established forever. Do as you promised, so that it will be established and that your name will be great forever" (1 Chron. 17:23–24). David declared God's promises, reviewed what God had said and established support for his argument with Scripture. Praying the Word is powerful!

As surely as God's house is a house of prayer, God's Word is a book of prayer. Prayer and Scripture are a dynamic duo! Prayer serves the Word, and the Word serves prayer. Prayer gives wings to the Word of God. Paul wrote, "Finally, brothers, pray for us that the message of the Lord may spread rapidly and be honored, just as it was with you" (2 Thess. 3:1).

The Word of God also authenticates our prayer. The psalmist said, "The unfolding of your words gives light; it gives understanding to the simple" (Ps. 119:130). Scripture needs to be planted in our hearts if we are to discern His will. It is impossible to be ignorant of the Word and proficient in prayer. We can more effectively communicate our desires in intercessory prayer when our hearts, minds and our prayers are filled with relevant Scripture.

Psalm 119 is the longest chapter of the longest book in the Bible. Although it was written to reveal the power and the beauty of the Word of God, the entire chapter is a prayer—all 176 verses! Effective prayer is so dependent upon and rooted in Scripture that Jesus said, "If you remain in me and my words remain in you, ask whatever you wish, and it will be given you" (John 15:7).

Case Preparation: Defending Others in Court

What the Judge has said (the written law) binds Him to act in a certain way. God is true to His Word! So, list the legal points that must be proven in order for you to prevail. Then search for and write out pertinent scriptures that back up your petition. It is the language of the court. A working knowledge of Scripture tells the Judge that you are familiar with the law. The advocate then confidently creates a valid story that enables the court to see how the evidence supports the facts and on which laws his appeal is based.

Understand court precedent

Precedent is determined by something said or done earlier that serves as an example. What God has done historically sets legal precedent. It indicates what He is likely to do in the future.

While in prayer, remind Him of His past accomplishments. Not because *He* tends to forget, but because *we* tend to forget. When we remind the Lord of what He has done in the past, it is proof that we remember Him! To remember His works is to honor Him! God says:

- "Remember the wonders he has done, his miracles, and the judgments he pronounced" (1 Chron. 16:12).

- "Remember to extol his work, which men have praised in song" (Job 36:24).

- "I will remember the deeds of the Lord; yes, I will remember your miracles of long ago" (Ps. 77:11).

We should remind the Lord of what He has done for us. What He has done for us in the past sets a precedent. After all, our God is a God who never changes! He promises, "I the LORD do not change. So you, O descendants of Jacob, are not destroyed" (Mal. 3:6). What a reassuring thought!

When you remind God of what He has done in the past,

include things He has done for others. Why? It's simple. Our Father is no respecter of persons. He does not prefer one of us above another, and He shows no favoritism. (See Acts 10:34; Colossians 3:25.)

The Judge's character

We prepare our petition with the facts, evidence, the law and historical precedent, and we plead it according to the Judge's character! His character is another guarantee we have in court. Our God is faithful!

David remembered God's integrity when he prayed:

> Righteousness and justice are the foundation of your throne; love and faithfulness go before you. Blessed are those who have learned to acclaim you, who walk in the light of your presence, O LORD. They rejoice in your name all day long; they exult in your righteousness. For you are their glory and strength, and by your favor you exalt our horn.
>
> —PSALM 89:14–17

Follow proper protocol before the Judge of heaven. Review His character qualities on which you base your appeal. The following statements contain only four of God's many wonderful character traits:

- "Lord, because of Your *tender love,* I ask You to..." (John 3:16)

- "Because of Your *amazing grace,* please..." (John 1:14, 16; Acts 20:24)

- "Because of Your *abundant mercy,* I request..." (James 2:13)

- "Because of Your *great faithfulness,* would You..." (Ps. 89:1; 119:90; Lam. 3:22–23)

Case Preparation: Defending Others in Court

God's *intentions* determine His actions. His intentions are always pure! What a blessing it is to know that He is "not willing that any should perish, but that all should come to repentance" and that His "mercy triumphs over judgment" (2 Pet. 3:9 KJV; James 2:13).

One of the many colorful characters who became legends of the American Old West was "Hanging Judge Roy Bean," who held court sessions in his saloon along the Rio Grande River in a desolate stretch of the Chihuahuan Desert of West Texas. Horse thieves dreaded being tried by Judge Bean because they knew the gallows was their next and last stop! To hear some people pray, you would think we serve a mean, punitive, abusive God who wants to abuse us. Not so! Our heavenly Father longs to show us His great love.

The prayer

Write out your request(s) as an attorney would write out his argument. Be specific, not vague. Ask the Lord for a decision in your favor or in favor of your client. James exhorts us that we sometimes ask and don't receive because we ask with wrong motives (James 4:3). Please note that when we ask for God's favor, we should also ask for His wisdom in the matter. Otherwise, we may suffer disappointment.

Clearly state your request, and thoroughly explain why you hold that position. Refer to the evidence, facts and applicable laws. It isn't enough to just talk to God about the situation. *Ask Him for something!*

As an example, we can rightly request forgiveness of our sins because the law (God's Word) says we can. We do so because we know that historically God has forgiven repentant sinners (precedent). We count on the fact that Christ shed His own blood for our sins (evidence). (See Matthew 6:12.)

While we were interviewing an attorney to collect information for writing this book, he said that some attorneys can't succinctly, specifically state their requests to the judge. In a recent trial, the judge met him and his opponent in chambers in order to decide the case.

The judge asked his opponent, "Sir, what is it that you are asking from me?"

The man answered angrily, "Well, Your Honor, they have done this and that, and they have said this and that."

Again the judge asked, "And what decision are you asking me to make?" Once again the man nervously stated another complaint. Bill, the lawyer telling us the story, said, "Eddie, the lawyer was never able to unplug from complaining and explaining long enough to tell the judge what he specifically wanted. As a result, the judge awarded me the case."

It is interesting to us that the phrase "She didn't have a prayer" is normally understood to be synonymous with "She didn't have a chance." In fact, she (or he) may have had a chance. The word *prayer* comes from an Old English word meaning "to ask, to request." It is a legal term. In fact, at the end of each lawsuit filed in Texas is the final subtitle: "The Prayer." Here is where the attorney is to specify what he is asking of the court. What the phrase "She didn't have a prayer" really means is, "She didn't make a request!"

In January 1994, my (Eddie) mother went to be with the Lord. She passed quietly in her sleep. She was a praying woman. She and my dad prayed together each night before they fell asleep. She would pray first, then he would pray. Rather than completely close her prayer, she would conclude with "in Jesus' name ... " and allow my father to add the "amen" at the close of his prayer.

The next morning as my father and I sought to comfort each other with Mom's passing, he reminded me, "The last words I heard your mother say were, "In Jesus' name."

Case Preparation: Defending Others in Court

The decision

Many years ago our friend Evangelist Manley Beasley lay dying in a Houston hospital. He had five diseases, and three of them were terminal. No one expected he would leave the hospital alive. Then one night while he read his Bible, God spoke to Manley. In a moment God transformed Psalm 128:6 (KJV), "Yea, thou shalt see thy children's children," from *logos* (God's general Word to everyone), into *rhema* (His specific Word for Manley).

Immediately Manley explained to the doctors and nurses that he would not die. Why? Because he had no grandchildren, and none of his children were married yet! At first the hospital staff humored him. Then to their amazement, Manley's body began to gain strength. Specialists from around the world came to witness the transformation. Not only did Manley Beasley leave the hospital, but he traveled the United States another twenty years and taught a powerful message of faith.

God's Word is immutable, irrevocable and eternal!

If you were to take someone's last will and testament to court, the judge would be required by law to honor it even if the deceased person had made a mistake in writing it. It doesn't even matter if the will makes sense to anyone. If the deceased leaves millions of dollars to his pet canary, the court must enforce it!

When we approach the bar of God on the basis of God's will and testament, whether it's His Old or New Testament, how much more God is obliged to act? Therefore, the Word strength of our prayers often determines heaven's response to them.

In Exodus 17 we read how Joshua's army fought the Amalekites. It says that as Joshua and his army fought in the valley below...

> Moses, Aaron, and Hur went up to the top of the hill. And it came to pass, when Moses held up his hand, that Israel prevailed: and when he let down his hand, Amalek prevailed. But Moses' hands were heavy; and they took a stone, and

put it under him, and he sat thereon; and Aaron and Hur stayed up his hands, the one on the one side, and the other on the other side; and his hands were steady until the going down of the sun. And Joshua discomfited Amalek and his people with the edge of the sword. And the LORD said unto Moses, Write this for a memorial in a book, and rehearse it in the ears of Joshua: for I will utterly put out the remembrance of Amalek from under heaven.

—EXODUS 17:10–14, KJV

The Lord even told Moses to write the event down as a testimony of His answers to Moses' prayer. Unfortunately, many of us have never seen the seriousness of the situation. As God's advocates it is our privilege to save lives, evangelize nations and perhaps shape history!

BIBLICAL DEFENSE ATTORNEYS AND THEIR CASES

Now that we have looked closely at these seven principles for preparing our cases for the heavenly court, let's see how several biblical defense attorneys used the principles in the cases they presented to the Judge. From each of these, we can learn how better to be prepared as defense attorney advocates/intercessors in our own world.

Moses' defense of the children of Israel (Exod. 32:11–14)

As we enter the courtroom, the attorney for Israel's defense, Moses, stands and approaches the bench. Let's listen and see what we can learn from his courtroom technique.

1. Moses stated the facts.

Moses very clearly stated the facts of his case to God. In essence, these facts included: "You are angry with us. You brought us out of Egypt. Now our enemies are questioning Your integrity."

> But Moses sought the favor of the LORD his God. "O
> LORD," he said, "why should your anger burn against your
> people, whom you brought out of Egypt with great power
> and a mighty hand? Why should the Egyptians say, 'It was
> with evil intent that he brought them out, to kill them in
> the mountains and to wipe them off the face of the earth'?"
>
> —Exodus 32:11–12

2. Moses offered the prayer.

This was a one-sentence request from Moses summarizing
what he was asking from God:

> Turn from your fierce anger; relent and do not bring
> disaster on your people.
>
> —Exodus 32:12

3. Moses quoted the law.

Moses reminded the Judge of what He said in His law:

> Remember your servants Abraham, Isaac and Israel, to
> whom you swore by your own self: "I will make your
> descendants as numerous as the stars in the sky and I will
> give your descendants all this land I promised them, and it
> will be their inheritance forever."
>
> —Exodus 32:13

4. Moses appealed to the Judge's character.

By reminding the Judge of His promises to Abraham, Isaac
and Israel, Moses was reminding God that His purposes for the
children of Israel were great and long reaching. Moses also
reminded the Judge of His own mighty deeds in protecting the
Israelites.

5. The Judge rendered the decision.

Moses won his case as God relented and did not bring disaster.

> Then the LORD relented and did not bring on his people the disaster he had threatened.
>
> —EXODUS 32:14

Jeremiah's defense of Israel (Jer. 14: 7, 10, 17–18, 19–21, 15:19)

If you know much about the Old Testament, you know that the children of Israel were continually being prosecuted for their crimes. In the fourteenth chapter of Jeremiah we find Jeremiah pleading a case for them. Notice how Jeremiah employs the same courtroom techniques that Moses used.

1. Jeremiah stated the facts.

Jeremiah honestly and humbly acknowledged the facts of his case before God:

> Although our sins testify against us, O LORD, do something for the sake of your name. For our backsliding is great; we have sinned against you.
>
> —JEREMIAH 14:7

2. Jeremiah produced the evidence.

The evidence for this case came directly from the testimony of the Lord concerning His people. God gave this evidence:

> This is what the LORD says about this people: "They greatly love to wander; they do not restrain their feet."
>
> —JEREMIAH 14:10

3. Jeremiah referred to the law.

God's law was very clear about the result of His people's

wandering ways: God will remember their wickedness and punish them.

> He will now remember their wickedness and punish them for their sins.
>
> —JEREMIAH 14:10

4. Jeremiah pleaded on the basis of court precedent.

In essence he said, "You haven't completely rejected Judah. You don't despise Zion. Therefore, heal us."

> Have you rejected Judah completely? Do you despise Zion? Why have you afflicted us so that we cannot be healed? We hoped for peace but no good has come, for a time of healing but there is only terror.
>
> —JEREMIAH 14:19

5. Jeremiah offered the prayer.

Jeremiah's prayer humbly acknowledged the wickedness and guilt of the people. He pleaded for God's favor and forgiveness:

> O LORD, we acknowledge our wickedness and the guilt of our fathers; we have indeed sinned against you. For the sake of your name do not despise us; do not dishonor your glorious throne. Remember your covenant with us and do not break it.
>
> —JEREMIAH 14:20–21

6. Judge Jehovah rendered the decision.

The Judge was very clear in His decision, stating, "If you repent, I will restore you that you may serve Me."

> Therefore this is what the LORD says: "If you repent, I will

restore you that you may serve me; if you utter worthy, not worthless, words, you will be my spokesman. Let this people turn to you, but you must not turn to them."

—Jeremiah 15:19

In this case, as happens from time to time, the Judge's decision was conditional and finally rested on the defendant's response. It was an "if/then" decision. (See 2 Chronicles 7:14).

Isaiah's prophetic plea (Isa. 15:1–3; 16:3–5)

Like the prophets before him, Isaiah knew how to plead a case in the court of heaven. Let's quietly slip into the courtroom and eavesdrop. Listen to what Isaiah, Israel's defense attorney, is saying.

1. Isaiah stated the facts.

> An oracle concerning Moab: Ar in Moab is ruined, destroyed in a night! Kir in Moab is ruined, destroyed in a night! Dibon goes up to its temple, to its high places to weep; Moab wails over Nebo and Medeba. Every head is shaved and every beard cut off.

—Isaiah 15:1–2

2. Isaiah presented the evidence.

Isaiah reported the evidence of the people's disobedience.

> In the streets they wear sackcloth; on the roofs and in the public squares they all wail, prostrate with weeping.

—Isaiah 15:3

3. Isaiah offered the prayer.

Isaiah pleaded in his prayer for God's counsel, asking Him to render a decision:

> Give us counsel, render a decision. Make your shadow
> like night—at high noon. Hide the fugitives, do not betray
> the refugees.
>
> —Isaiah 16:3

4. Isaiah elaborated on the prayer.

> Let the Moabite fugitives stay with you; be their shelter
> from the destroyer. The oppressor will come to an end,
> and destruction will cease; the aggressor will vanish from
> the land.
>
> —Isaiah 16:4

5. The Judge rendered the decision.

The Judge predicted the outcome of His decision: "The oppressor will come to an end, destruction will cease... one who in judging seeks justice and speeds the cause of righteousness" (vv. 4–5).

> In love a throne will be established; in faithfulness a man
> will sit on it—one from the house of David—one who in
> judging seeks justice and speeds the cause of righteousness.
>
> —Isaiah 16:5

MY STORY

I (Alice) have learned to incorporate these principles in my own life. The following illustration will demonstrate how I used the prayer pattern of the prophets in an incident involving our son. Several years ago our second son was out late one night. Exhausted from the heavy workload that day, we went to bed. Around 3:00 in the morning, I sat straight up in the bed, alarmed with a sense of danger. I checked Bryan's room and realized he was not home. I began to intercede for him, because I knew something was wrong for him not to be home—or even call home. I immediately began presenting my case to my heavenly Judge, using the principles I had learned from God's Word.

1.   The facts

Bryan was not home, and we had not received a call from him.

> Father, Your promise to me for Bryan is found in Psalm 27:2–3: "When evil men advance against [Bryan] to devour [his] flesh, when [his] enemies and [his] foes attack [him], they will stumble and fall. Though an army besiege [him], [his] heart [and mine] will not fear; though war break out against [him], even then will [he] be confident."

2.   The evidence

I awoke with intercession in my heart. I was alerted by the Lord, as a watchman on the wall for Bryan.

> Lord Jesus, I pray for Bryan right now that You will "preserve sound judgment and discernment, do not let [him] out of your sight…be life for [him], an ornament to grace [his] neck. Then [he] will go on [his] way in safety, and [Bryan's] foot will not stumble; when [he] lies down, [he] will not be afraid… [his] sleep will be sweet." According to Your Word as revealed in Proverbs 3:21–24, I declare his safety.

3.   The law

I reminded God, "Bryan loves You and wants to obey Your commands."

> Father, I remind You of Your Word for those who love You. In Psalm 119:165–168, You assure me that "great peace have they who love your law, and nothing can make them stumble. I wait for your salvation, O Lord,

and I follow your commands. [Bryan and I] obey your statutes, for [we] love them greatly. [We] obey your precepts and your statutes, for all [our] ways are known to you."

4.   The precedent

In 1985, God had given me a scripture for our four children, and I clung to His promise.

> Father in heaven, You have promised to keep Your covenant with Israel. You will do the same with me because You are a Father of covenants. Your law says, "Not one of all the Lord's good promises to the house of Israel failed; every one was fulfilled" (Josh. 21:45).

5.   The Judge's character

Our heavenly Father wants to fulfill His purpose of our lives. As a defender for our son, I called on the great character of Jehovah.

> Father, how wonderful it is to realize You are so gracious in all Your ways. According to Psalm 17:7, please "show the wonder of your great love, you who save by your right hand those who take refuge in you from their foes."

6.   The prayer

I was now entering the courts of heaven to plead Bryan's case.

> Lord, I don't know what has happened to Bryan, but I am asking for Your divine mercy. As his attorney in prayer, I ask You to "remember, O LORD, your great mercy and love, for they are from old. Remember not the sins of [his] youth and [his] rebellious ways; according to your love remember [him], for you are

good, O Lord. Good and upright is the Lord; therefore [You] instruct sinners in [Your] ways" (Ps. 25:6–8). Lord, I am asking for Bryan's safe return, a renewed peace of mind that You are with him and an assurance that You are guarding him all the days of his life.

7. The decision

Once we plead our case, we release it until the burden returns. About four hours later Bryan came in a little shaken up. He had taken a new friend home and tried taking a shortcut while coming home, only to get lost. Once he tried to turn around in the road, his car got stuck in the mud.

He decided to wait until morning, locked the car doors and tried to fall asleep. The night was very dark. Some curious strangers driving by apparently entertained the thought of doing mischief with Bryan's car, slowed down and evaluated the situation, but then continued on. When morning arrived, Bryan got help from one of the very few travelers on that unfamiliar road by pushing his stuck car out of the mud. The Lord protected him that night. I won my case. The Judge's gavel had fallen, and He declared, "It is done." Bryan came home safe and sound.

Now it is time for you to practice your own case preparation. The assignment on the following pages will give you an opportunity to apply these principles to each matter of intercession to which you commit in your role as advocate with the people in your life. Use the pages to develop your case for presentation to Judge Jehovah.

We are too busy to pray, and so we are too busy to have power. We have a great deal of activity, but we accomplish little; many services but few conversions; much machinery but few results.
—R. A. Torrey

Case Preparation: Defending Others in Court

ASSIGNMENT

1. List your prayer assignments.

2. Make copies of the "Case Preparation Sheet."

3. Complete each category as much as possible.

4. Study Scripture as it pertains to each case and continue building your arguments.

5. Utilize the sheet as you pray purposely and faithfully to the Judge of heaven!

Advocate's Case Preparation Sheet for the Court of Heaven

Date: _____

Client: _____

The person(s) or issue you are representing in prayer. ("I am praying for...")

The Facts: (Both the physical and spiritual facts as you believe them to be.)

1) _____

2) _____

3) _____

4) _____

5) _____

The Evidence: (Reasons to believe these to be the facts. Include things you've seen, heard, experienced or received as a revelation from God. Revelation doesn't establish fact, but it can serve as evidence that something is a fact.)

1) _____

2) _____

3) _____

4) _____

5) _____

The Law: (Scripture that addresses the issue directly or indirectly.)

1) _____

2) _____

3) _____

4) _____

5) _____

Precedent: (Past actions God has taken on your or someone else's behalf that might indicate what He is likely to do again. These include actions He has taken throughout your life and throughout history. Search the Scriptures.)

1) _____

2) _____

3) _____

4) _____

5) _____

The Judge's Character: (Facts about God and His character of which you will remind yourself constantly.)

1) _____

2) _____

3) _____

4) _____

5) _____

The Prayer: (State simply and specifically what you are asking of God. "On the basis of the evidence, the law and what You have done in the past, I am asking You, Eternal Judge of heaven, to grant the following...")

1) _____

2) _____

3) _____

4) _____

5) _____

The Decision: (Record the decision of the court—any answers the Lord has given you regarding this intercessory assignment.)

1) _____

2) _____

3) _____

4) _____

5) _____

The Appeal: (Sometimes after God denies a request, we may resubmit it. For examples see Exodus 32:7–14; 2 Samuel 24; Psalm 106:6–31, 44–45; Jeremiah 26:10–19; Luke 11:5–13; 18:1–8)

1) _____

2) _____

3) _____

4) _____

5) _____

Chapter 9

Win or Lose?

*Prayer does not mean that I am to bring God
down to my thoughts and my purposes and bend His
government according to my foolish, silly and sometimes
sinful notions. Prayer means that I am to be raised up into
feeling, into union and design with Him; that I am to enter
into His counsel and carry out His purpose fully.*
—Dwight L. Moody

GENE Stallings tells of an incident when he was defensive backfield coach of the Dallas Cowboys' football team. Two All-Pro players, Charlie Waters and Cliff Harris, were sitting in front of their lockers after playing a tough game against the Washington Redskins. They were still in their uniforms, and their heads were bowed in exhaustion. Waters said to Harris, "By the way, Cliff, what was the final score?"[1]

As these men show, excellence isn't determined by comparing our score to someone else's. Excellence comes from giving our best, no matter the score! And there are several things that can make the difference between winning and losing our cases in court. The most important issue is to approach our case with a spirit of excellence.

KEYS TO WINNING OUR CASE

Here are some keys to use to insure winning our case.

Divine timing

Although there is no right way to do the wrong thing, there are a myriad of wrong ways to do the right thing. Most frequently, the wrong way to do the right thing is to do it at the wrong time!

To argue a case in prayer successfully and win a decision, we must learn the significance of God's timing. Timing is everything! With most things there is a window of opportunity. As they say, "If you snooze, you lose!" In war, firepower is wasted if unleashed in the wrong time sequence.

Of David's military might, perhaps no other group was as important as the "men of Issachar, who understood the times and knew what Israel should do" (1 Chron. 12:32). May we become "men of Issachar" who understand the times and seasons of God. As intimates of God, we can be trusted with His secrets. "The Lord confides in those who fear him; he makes his covenant known to them" (Ps. 25:14).

Many years ago while in prayer, the Lord told us that we could have as much of Him as we wanted. If we are willing to sacrifice the time in prayer, we can have more of God. This will increase our ability to hear His voice and know His ways. This will improve our ability to plead our cases according to the right timing. As in times of war, our intercessory prayers can be timed as effectively as a nuclear warhead hitting the target.

Persistence

Dwight L. Moody once said, "Some people think God does not like to be troubled with our constant coming and asking. The way to trouble God is not to come at all."

We must learn persistence. God tells us, "Ask and it will be given to you; seek and you will find; knock and the door will be opened to you" (Matt. 7:7). The three words *ask, seek* and *knock* (in the original Greek) all carry the idea of continuance. We don't ask, seek, or knock once. How long do I strive? Prepare to return to the courtroom (the place of prayer) again and again to submit your case until the Judge decides in your favor or until Jesus Christ, your lead attorney, releases you from this case.

Sometimes the Lord is monitoring our tenacity and our persistence in prayer. So an appeal to God might be in order if the expected verdict was not achieved. In legal terms, an *appeal* is when the case has been reviewed, restructured and then reheard by the judge with a stronger intention for vindication.

Satan, our adversary, doesn't quit easily either. He will usually appeal any case he loses. He is a master of intimidation. Even after you have won a case, he may challenge your victory again and again, so be ready for a counterattack. Don't give in to his schemes!

However, when we strive too long about an issue we can easily move from *persistence* to *presumption*. Usually our spirit-man is uncomfortable praying for these matters. God keeps His assignments alive in our hearts until we have won the victory in the heavenlies. When the victory is realized, faith is complete in us. Our inner man is rested, the battle is over and our confidence is secure.

Hebrews 11:1–2 reminds us that faith is an unseen activity where our heart and God's heart have made a covenant of victory. Colossians 3:15 says, "And let the peace of God rule in your hearts..." The word *rule* is the Greek word *brabeuo,* which means "to umpire, arbitrate, direct or govern."

In our American game of baseball the umpire watches a runner slide carefully into home plate attempting to score. There are times when it is obvious that the runner is safe at home. The umpire bellows loudly, "SAFE!" On other occasions, the umpire declares to the runner and all those watching that he is "OUT!" No score given! The Holy Spirit is our Umpire who will govern our spirit. He will confirm or reject the ongoing need to pray about an issue. We can trust Him—He is our built-in Umpire! Or as the tribal wisdom of the Dakota Indians puts it, "When the horse dies, dismount!"

Specificity

To be successful in the courtroom as well as in prayer, we must learn to be specific. Praying in vague generalities produces little or nothing. As James wrote, "You do not have, because you do not ask God. When you ask, you do not receive, because you ask with wrong motives, that you may spend what you get on your pleasures" (James 4:2–3).

Some of us ask so generally that if God were to answer our prayer specifically, we wouldn't recognize it! For example, when we are faced with a need for $5,000, we pray for God to bless us. And He does! No, we don't get the $5,000, but we are blessed with beautiful children, good health and a great job. By the world's standards we have an abundance of food to eat. But where's the $5,000? We never really specifically asked.

Some ask, "Since God knows that we need $5,000, why must we ask?"

We ask because He commands us to ask. We ask in order to proclaim Him as our direct supplier.

Once I (Eddie) was asked where the money comes from that enables us to operate the ministry of the U.S. PRAYER CENTER.

"Do you know where it comes from?" a man asked.

"Of course I know where it comes from," I answered. Pointing upward I continued, "It always comes from the same place. He just uses many different routes to get it here!"

A serious problem in the church today is not asking God for anything, only talking to Him. If you want breakthrough, don't beat around the bush. Don't just converse with the Lord about your situation. Ask Him directly for what you need or want! And expect an answer! Don't be like the church members who prayed for rain, but showed up for the next service without umbrellas!

Fervency

One often-overlooked key to answered prayer is the issue of fervency. There is little fervency because of our failure to be specific. Fervency requires specificity! We can't be passionate about that which is uncertain. It is time for passion to permeate our intercession. One of the most passionate, fervent prayers ever prayed was the prayer Moses prayed for the children of Israel. He argued as a defense attorney in the court of God, and he won the case!

An example of an advocate fervently pleading and winning a case was Elijah atop Mount Carmel. After defeating the four hundred fifty prophets of Baal, Elijah didn't leave the mountaintop. Why? It's simple—Elijah had not come there simply to kill Baal's prophets. He had climbed that mountain to see rain end a three-year draught.

Then Elijah commanded them, "Seize the prophets of Baal. Don't let anyone get away!" They seized them, and Elijah had them brought down to the Kishon Valley and slaughtered there.

And Elijah said to Ahab, "Go, eat and drink, for there is the sound of a heavy rain." So Ahab went off to eat and drink, but Elijah climbed to the top of Carmel, bent down to the ground and put his face between his knees.

"Go and look toward the sea," he told his servant. And he went up and looked.

"There is nothing there," he said.

Seven times Elijah said, "Go back."

The seventh time the servant reported, "A cloud as small as a man's hand is rising from the sea."

So Elijah said, "Go and tell Ahab, 'Hitch up your chariot and go down before the rain stops you.'"

Meanwhile, the sky grew black with clouds, the wind rose, a heavy rain came on and Ahab rode off to Jezreel.

—1 Kings 18:40–45

Elijah was acting upon a promise he had received from God in the first verse. "After a long time, in the third year, the word of the LORD came to Elijah: 'Go and present yourself to Ahab, and I will send rain on the land'"(1 Kings 18:1). We must learn God's promises, hear His promises and act upon them in fervent faith.

BUILDING THE ALTAR

James wrote, "The prayer of a righteous man is powerful and effective. Elijah was a man just like us. He prayed earnestly that it would not rain, and it did not rain on the land for three and a half years. Again he prayed, and the heavens gave rain, and the earth produced its crops" (James 5:16–18). Who wouldn't want to have a prayer life like that!

Let's take another a closer look at Elijah's prayer. Or more specifically, *his preparation!*

In the eighteenth chapter of 1 Kings, which we looked at in the preceding section, Elijah watched the prophets of Baal pray and cry out to their false god until the time for the evening sacrifice. But there was no response—no one answered, no one paid attention.

Then Elijah built an altar of twelve stones, one for each of the tribes of Jacob, and dug a large trench around it. Next he arranged firewood on the altar, cut a bull into pieces and laid the parts on the wood. Then Elijah had servants fill four large jars with water and instructed them to pour it on the offering and on the wood three times! The water ran down around the altar and filled the trench. At the time of sacrifice, the prophet Elijah stepped forward and prayed:

> O LORD, God of Abraham, Isaac and Israel, let it be known today that you are God in Israel and that I am your servant and have done all these things at your command. Answer me, O LORD, answer me, so these people will know that you, O LORD, are God, and that you are turning their hearts back again.
>
> —1 KINGS 18:36–37

At that moment the fire of the Lord fell and burned up the sacrifice, the wood, the stones and the soil and licked up the water in the trench as well. When the people saw this miracle they fell down and cried, "The LORD—he is God!" (v. 39).

Notice the words Elijah prayed. "I have done all these things at your command." All *what* things? Elijah followed the Lord's instructions to prepare. The fire of God didn't fall until the stones were in place, the wood assembled, the sacrifice ready and the water poured out. Water is representative of the Word of God (Eph. 5:26). *Only then* did God answer! When we get into the Word and get the Word into us, we can begin to pray more effectively and expect God to answer! Isaiah 55:11 says, "So shall my word be that goeth forth out of my mouth: it shall not return unto me void, but it shall accomplish that which I please, and it shall prosper in the thing whereto I sent it" (KJV). God's Word simply cannot fail.

God doesn't show up until the stage is set. We must stop long enough to build the altar and cover it with water if we expect to see the fire fall! Our victories will be in question until we first prepare our altar and ourselves. If you are one who is always in search of someone to pray for you, it could be a sign that you are a *Word*less warrior. You have not stopped long enough to collect the stones to build your own altar. Unfortunately, some of us live our lives leaning on the altars of others instead of building our own altars of sacrifice. You want fire from heaven? Then present an acceptable sacrifice to God (Eph. 6:13–14).

THE POWER OF AN ADVOCATE'S INTERCESSORY PRAYER

It is reported that George Muller was a man who understood the price of intercession. In his diary, this mighty man of prayer had recorded over fifty thousand answers to his prayers at the time of his death. But one answer to prayer was yet to come.

Muller said this: "The great point is never to give up until the answer comes. I have been praying for sixty-three years and eight months for one man's conversion. He is not saved yet, but he will be. How can it be otherwise . . . I am praying."

The day came when Muller's friend received Christ. It did not come until Muller's casket was lowered in the ground. There, near an open grave, this friend gave his heart to God. Prayers of perseverance had won another battle. Muller's success may be summarized in four powerful words: *He did not quit.*[2]

Stories like this inspire and encourage us to keep praying. God does hear and answer His praying people.

PERSONAL REQUESTS

One of the boldest prayers anyone ever prayed is Jabez' prayer, contained in a single verse:

> Jabez cried out to the God of Israel, "Oh, that you would bless me and enlarge my territory! Let your hand be with me, and keep me from harm so that I will be free from pain." And God granted his request.
>
> —1 CHRONICLES 4:10

God granted his request! The Hebrew name *Jabez* means "sorrow or pain." This man mentioned in the Bible was without a family connection, but we know his mother bore him in sorrow. She might have delivered Jabez at the time she was widowed or out of wedlock, or she may have even died in childbirth. Scripture does not say. The important thing about this man Jabez is that he cried out to God, and God heard and answered him. Look at the four things Jabez asked of God.

- Bless me indeed (financial provision)
- Enlarge my boundaries (increased sphere of influence)
- Let Your hand be with me (increased anointing and authority)
- Deliver me from evil (protection from the schemes of the enemy)

These general requests are ones that God hears from us the most often. We are encouraged to know that God heard Jabez, and we have every right to believe that He hears the cry of our hearts as well.

ANSWERS TO SINCERE PRAYERS

We are heartened to know that our gracious God even hears the prayers of sincere seekers! Dr. Luke wrote:

> At Caesarea there was a man named Cornelius, a centurion in what was known as the Italian Regiment. He and all his family were devout and God-fearing; he gave generously to those in need and prayed to God regularly. One day at about three in the afternoon he had a vision. He distinctly saw an angel of God, who came to him and said, "Cornelius!"
>
> Cornelius stared at him in fear. "What is it, Lord?" he asked.
>
> The angel answered, "Your prayers and gifts to the poor have come up as a memorial offering before God."
>
> —Acts 10:1–4

Later in the chapter, Cornelius and his entire family received Christ and followed Him in baptism! God honored the prayers of this humble man.

LAST-MINUTE ANSWERS

Experts tell us that the 911 emergency system is state-of-the-art technology. All you need do is dial those numbers, and you will almost instantly be connected to a dispatcher. The computer monitor in front of the dispatcher will display your telephone number, your address and the name by which that telephone number is listed at that address.

A caller might not be able to state specifically what the problem is. Perhaps a woman's husband has just suffered a heart attack, and she is so out of control that all she can do is hysterically scream into the telephone. But the dispatcher doesn't need her to say anything. He knows where the call is coming from. Help is already on the way.

Win or Lose?

There come times in our lives when, in our desperation and pain, we dial 911 prayers. Sometimes we're hysterical. Sometimes we don't know the words to speak. But God hears. He knows our name and our circumstance. Help is on the way; God has already begun to bring the remedy.[3]

Jesus heard and answered last-minute prayers even when He was dying:

> One of the criminals who hung there hurled insults at him: "Aren't you the Christ? Save yourself and us!"
>
> But the other criminal rebuked him. "Don't you fear God," he said, "since you are under the same sentence? We are punished justly, for we are getting what our deeds deserve. But this man has done nothing wrong."
>
> Then he said, "Jesus, remember me when you come into your kingdom."
>
> Jesus answered him, "I tell you the truth, today you will be with me in paradise."
>
> —LUKE 23:39–43

KEYS TO UNDERSTAND

When we complain to God in prayer about Satan's treatment, and heaven is silent, it may be that we have not effectively stated our case, presented our evidence, pointed out the law that has been or is being violated in order to bring charges against the perpetrator! All the while, as we gripe and moan about our circumstances, God is saying, "Review the past for me, let us argue the matter together; state the case for your innocence" (Isa. 43:26).

The Lord is not as moved by our tears as He is moved by our faith when it is based on His Word (Rom. 10:17, KJV). It's not that we shouldn't be emotional, but the foundation of our prayer should be God's Truth, not our feelings! Faith is our greatest advantage in prayer (Heb. 11:6).

It stands to reason that God's answers would not be forthcoming to those who don't believe that He exists. But we are amazed at how many Christians believe that God is, but doubt that He loves them enough to give them what they earnestly seek.

Without proper preparation, no lawyer can expect to win his case. Remember, he will make a fool of himself before the judge, his client, his adversary and the gallery! Many of us do not receive the answers we want when we pray simply because we have not properly prepared to pray.

In John 11 Jesus was informed of His friend Lazarus's impending death. You may recall that Jesus stayed where He was for two more days after He was told of Lazarus's illness. Why? Because He knew that Lazarus needed a resurrection! Jesus also knew that He had to win the victory in heaven's courtroom before it would be manifested in the streets. He stayed to prepare His case, present it before Judge Jehovah and win the decision.

When Jesus arrived at Bethany, He found that Lazarus had already been in the tomb for four days. He asked, "Where have you laid him?"

"Come and see, Lord," they replied. John 11:35, the shortest verse in the Bible, tells us that Jesus wept when He stood before His friend's tomb.

Then Jesus instructed the servants to take away the stone. He looked up into heaven and said, "Father, I thank You that You have heard Me."

"You have *heard* me?" What did Jesus say? What was He talking about? When did the Father hear Him? We believe the Father heard Jesus during the two days that Jesus waited before He came to Bethany. During those two days He presented His case before the Judge, was assured of victory in His heart and won the case. The work had been done before Jesus arrived on the scene. The transaction had taken place on the altar of preparation. The only thing left to do was to read the verdict, decree it done and witness the manifestation!

So Jesus called in a loud voice, "Lazarus, come out!" And Lazarus came out, his hands and feet wrapped with strips of linen and a cloth around his face. Jesus then said to them, "Take off his grave clothes and let him go." And it says that many of the Jews who had seen what Jesus did believed on Him.

Like an attorney, we have building blocks or tools that we can use to develop the cases we will plead in court. Because an attorney knows that his presentation in court will either establish or reduce his credibility, he will spend far more time in preparation than he spends in presentation. Believe it! Satan our adversary knows whether or not we are credible when we stand as an advocate before the court of heaven.

WHEN LAWS COLLIDE

Almost every week we board an airplane to travel to some part of the world on a teaching assignment. Countless times we have experienced the collision of two of God's laws—the law of gravity and the law of aerodynamics. As the plane taxis down the runway, it reaches a speed at which these two laws collide. The result? The higher law takes over. Because the law of aerodynamics is higher, the plane defies the law of gravity and takes flight. It never ceases to amaze us!

Many of us today are more familiar with God's *deeds* than we are His *ways.* In Psalm 103:7 we read, "He [God] made known his ways to Moses, his deeds to the people of Israel." One of the more misunderstood ways of God has to do with His glory. We mistakenly believe that God puts our well-being above all things. Not so! Although our well-being is near to our Father's heart, it's definitely secondary to the glory of His name. Whenever there is a collision between His supplying a need we have and His own glory, God glorifies His name!

This is reflected in Paul's personal experience. He recalls, "To keep me from becoming conceited because of these surpassingly great revelations, there was given me a thorn in my flesh, a messenger of Satan, to torment me. Three times I pleaded with the Lord to take it away from me. But he said to me, 'My grace is sufficient for you, for my power is made perfect in weakness.' Therefore I will boast all the more gladly about my weaknesses, so that Christ's power may rest on me" (2 Cor. 12:7–9).

It is true that God desires for each one of us to be free. "Then you will know the truth, and the truth will set you free" (John 8:32). However, Paul was not granted his freedom though he prayed persistently ("three times") and passionately ("I pleaded with the Lord"). Although God didn't set Paul free from this messenger of Satan, He did extend to him sufficient grace so that the greater law was actually fulfilled in Paul's weakness!

If we don't know how to pray, we might actually pray for someone to be set free from a God-ordained circumstance. That's why we must seek to discern the facts before we take action on more serious prayer issues. We never want to pray contrary to God's will.

THINGS ARE NOT ALWAYS WHAT THEY SEEM

Does it bring greater glory to God when God saves a committed Christian from an agonizing execution or when God allows that person's martyrdom? In Acts 7, Stephen faced execution. One could have prayed for Stephen's safety, but in Stephen's case his martyrdom rather than his safety was judged to bring the higher glory to God. Stephen's death was not a matter of his being in the wrong place at the wrong time. It was not due to his unbelief—or even as a result of unconfessed sin. At times these things do keep our prayers from being answered. Yet Stephen simply died for the sake of Christ's glory. "Precious in the sight of the Lord is the death of his saints" (Ps. 116:15).

THE APPEAL

To *appeal a case* is to ask the Judge to overturn a former court decision. Throughout Scripture many successful appeals were made. The widow woman had no advantages with money, influence or favor. Yet she was tenacious in her pursuit of justice. In Luke 18:1–8, we read how God honored her appeal:

> Then Jesus told his disciples a parable to show them that they should always pray and not give up. He said: "In a certain town there was a judge who neither feared God nor cared about men. And there was a widow in that town who kept coming to him with the plea, 'Grant me justice against my adversary.'
>
> "For some time he refused. But finally he said to himself, 'Even though I don't fear God or care about men, yet because this widow keeps bothering me, I will see that she gets justice, so that she won't eventually wear me out with her coming!'"
>
> And the Lord said, "Listen to what the unjust judge says. And will not God bring about justice for his chosen ones, who cry out to him day and night? Will he keep putting them off? I tell you, he will see that they get justice, and quickly."

You may have been taught that to make the same request twice in prayer is unbelief. That simply isn't the case. In fact, Jesus teaches us here that God's decisions in our favor sometimes rest on our willingness to persevere in prayer.

David Bryant writes in *The Lighthouse Devotional:*

> At Oxford University three statues stand side by side. The first figure is seated with head in hands, thinking of things

eternal. The second is kneeling with hands clasped and arms outstretched toward heaven. The third figure stands erect, with shield and sword, ready to do battle. They represent the three key aspects of prayer: solidarity, advocacy and pursuit.

The seated statue demonstrates that part of intercession is coming into agreement with God, pondering what He wants, and then desire it with Him—*solidarity* with God. The kneeling figure represents our pleading with the Father on behalf of situations or people where others will not or cannot pray—*advocating* for them to God. The third figure represents God calling us into battle to press His purposes forward with unflagging zeal until we see accomplished what He has burdened us to pray for. This is where *pursuing* prayer takes over.

Jesus highlights these intensifying paces of intercession when He talks about "asking," agreeing with God and wanting it with Him; "seeking," when, like a lawyer, we seek God's best on behalf of others; and "knocking"— clearly the most aggressive and the most demanding of the three—when we're in pursuit of answers."[4]

In another example from Scripture, Jesus said:

Suppose one of you has a friend, and he goes to him at midnight and says, "Friend, lend me three loaves of bread, because a friend of mine on a journey has come to me, and I have nothing to set before him."

Then the one inside answers, "Don't bother me. The door is already locked, and my children are with me in bed. I can't get up and give you anything." I tell you, though he will not get up and give him the bread because he is his friend, yet because of the man's boldness he will get up and give him as much as he needs.

> So I say to you: Ask and it will be given to you; seek and you will find; knock and the door will be opened to you. For everyone who asks receives; he who seeks finds; and to him who knocks, the door will be opened.
>
> —Luke 11:5–10

Our heavenly Father sometimes waits to see the determination in our heart, our perseverance and tenacity before rendering a decision in our favor. But how do we know when we have heard His *final answer?* This is a difficult issue to decide. The best answer is to "let the peace of Christ rule in your hearts" (Col. 3:15). In John 16:13, Jesus teaches us that "when he, the Spirit of truth, comes, he will guide you into all truth." If the Holy Spirit lives in you, and you are listening to Him, it will be clear to your spirit that you have permission to keep pleading your case. If, when you pray for the same request, there is ever a sense of violation in your heart, then it is time to stop.

SCRIPTURE: THE LANGUAGE OF THE COURT

The following scriptures may help you state your case before the Lord. We are not trying to develop a ritual or standard that suggests that the Lord won't hear us otherwise. We do believe that Scripture clearly teaches us to prepare and to pray with purpose, as one would argue a case in court.

> His children are far from safety, crushed in court without a defender.
>
> —Job 5:4

> But if it were I, I would appeal to God; I would lay my cause before him.
>
> —Job 5:8

> Though I were innocent, I could not answer him; I could only plead with my Judge for mercy. Even if I summoned

him and he responded, I do not believe he would give me a hearing.

—Job 9:15–16

O earth, do not cover my blood; may my cry never be laid to rest! Even now my witness is in heaven; my advocate is on high. My intercessor is my friend as my eyes pour out tears to God; on behalf of a man he pleads with God as a man pleads for his friend.

—Job 16:18–21

Arise, O Lord, in your anger; rise up against the rage of my enemies. Awake, my God; decree justice.

—Psalm 7:6

Vindicate me, O God, and plead my cause against an ungodly nation; rescue me from deceitful and wicked men.

—Psalm 43:1

Rise up, O God, and defend your cause; remember how fools mock you all day long. Do not ignore the clamor of your adversaries, the uproar of your enemies, which rises continually.

—Psalm 74:22–23

When I was in distress, I sought the Lord; at night I stretched out untiring hands and my soul refused to be comforted.

—Psalm 77:2

"Has God forgotten to be merciful? Has he in anger withheld his compassion?" Then I thought, "To this I will appeal: the years of the right hand of the Most High."

—Psalm 77:9–10

Win or Lose?

God presides in the great assembly; he gives judgment among the "gods": How long will you defend the unjust and show partiality to the wicked? Defend the cause of the weak and fatherless; maintain the rights of the poor and oppressed.

—Psalm 82:1–2

Defend my cause and redeem me; preserve my life according to your promise.

—Psalm 119:154

Do not exploit the poor because they are poor and do not crush the needy in court, for the Lord will take up their case and will plunder those who plunder them.

—Proverbs 22:22–23

Speak up for those who cannot speak for themselves, for the rights of all who are destitute. Speak up and judge fairly; defend the rights of the poor and needy.

—Proverbs 31:8–9

Learn to do right! Seek justice, encourage the oppressed. Defend the cause of the fatherless, plead the case of the widow.

—Isaiah 1:17

It will be a sign and witness to the Lord Almighty in the land of Egypt. When they cry out to the Lord because of their oppressors, he will send them a savior and defender, and he will rescue them.

—Isaiah 19:20

The ruthless will vanish, the mockers will disappear, and all who have an eye for evil will be cut down—those who with a word make a man out to be guilty, who ensnare the defender in court and with false testimony deprive the innocent of justice.

—Isaiah 29:20–21

"Present your case," says the Lord. "Set forth your arguments," says Jacob's King.

—Isaiah 41:21

Review the past for me, let us argue the matter together; state the case for your innocence.

—Isaiah 43:26

No one calls for justice; no one pleads his case with integrity. They rely on empty arguments and speak lies; they conceive trouble and give birth to evil.

—Isaiah 59:4

Prayer is the easiest and hardest of all things;
the simplest and the sublimest; the weakest and the most
powerful; its results lie outside the range of human
possibilities; they are limited only by the omnipotence of God.
—E. M. Bounds

Chapter 10

Warfare Prayer: Prosecuting Satan in Court

*A praying saint performs far more havoc among
the unseen forces of darkness than we have the
slightest notion of.*

—Oswald Chambers

FOR eons a cosmic battle has raged between God and His former angel Lucifer (Satan). It is a battle for worshipers. One doesn't decide whether or not to *do* spiritual warfare. We were all born on a spiritual battlefield. The war rages around us incessantly. And, we were born POWs (prisoners of war)! Charles Finney was familiar with this war.

> A friend of Charles Finney tells about a man who came to Mr. Finney and said, "I don't believe in the existence of a devil."
>
> "Don't you?" said Finney. "Well, you resist him for a while, and you will believe in him."[1]

It is by being born again that we are rescued, recruited and released to fight our former oppressor. Paul taught the Ephesian Christians: "As for you, you were dead in your transgressions and sins, in which you used to live when you followed the ways of this world and of the ruler of the kingdom of the air, the spirit who is now at work in those who are disobedient" (Eph. 2:1–2).

The fighting we are to do is to be done in a court of law. (See Job 1:6–8; Revelation 12:10.) It is in this courtroom that we, as spiritual prosecuting attorneys under the leadership of our lead attorney, Jesus Christ, are to level our charges against the ancient outlaw Satan. This is spiritual warfare.

The American church has begun to realize that the devil and his demons are a real threat. But we must equip ourselves with the proper understanding, techniques and strategies to face him in court.

We have discussed our role as defense attorneys. In this chapter we will discuss our role as prosecuting attorneys. In jurisprudence, a *prosecutor* is an attorney who represents the government by presenting evidence to convict one who is charged with a crime. However, the prosecutor can only present evidence that the court allows. Without using the law, precedent of the court or proving otherwise, the judge will have no other choice but to rule against the prosecutor when he violates protocol. In a court of law, there are procedures and protocol that we must follow. There are strict methods of handling evidence so that it is not contaminated or misrepresented.

In our spiritual application, we represent the government of God. As prosecutors we identify where Satan has broken God's laws and prosecute him and his strongmen based on our covenant relationship with the Lord Jesus. As in any legal case where the prosecutor is held to strict codes, we can do no less. We must not represent or mishandle the opportunities God has given us to prosecute an ancient depraved deity. His crimes are very real—and we must be prepared and ready to prosecute him in court.

How many times have we seen someone engage in spiritual warfare with little or no biblical basis for his or her case?

For example, about a year ago we received a call from a distraught and confused pastor. Several of his church members, along with others from various denominations, formed a city prayer group. They decided on a way to destroy the principalities over their city. They invited the territorial spirits to enter a designated person in their group (with her full approval). Thinking they were in full control of the situation, they assumed they had cast the principalities that had entered the woman out of the city.

Friends, God is not within a million miles of this kind of foolishness! The group eventually dissolved, but the precious woman who as a medium "received" the spirits is still in bondage. Today she suffers from a martyr complex, convinced that having served Christ in this way is saving her city from evil. This is simply not biblical.

If you have been involved with this kind of activity, repent to the Lord right now. Then aloud, and with your eyes open, renounce and break all contracts, covenants or alliances you made with the powers of darkness in the process.

What about the times when evidence was disallowed in court because it was not presented at the right time or in the correct manner?

Seven churches in a beautiful U.S. city sponsored us to teach a citywide spiritual warfare conference. As our hosts drove us from the airport to the hotel, they began to list the territorial spirits they had dislodged and defeated in the past few years. They named pornography, among a handful of others. But as we drove through the streets, we couldn't help but notice the "gentlemen's clubs" (strip joints), dirty book shops, massage parlors and more. It was clear to us that they hadn't even stirred up much dust in the heavenlies concerning pornography.

God desires to see His kingdom come in every city. That is why Jesus told us to pray for it. Rather than spending hours railing against the demonic, it would be wiser for us to repent. The church can't pull down demonic strongholds with one hand that she holds up with the other. The church in America reflects almost every sin in American society. We must first repent, reconcile with God and each other, and then pray prayers of replacement, asking God to replace pride with humility, pornography with purity, anger with love or lies with truth. We believe that a time will come when a purified, unified church is assigned the task to assault the gates of hell. But timing is everything in these ambassadorial assignments. (See 2 Corinthians 5:20.)

We were in Ecuador several years ago. Intercession and spiritual warfare were in their infancy in the country at the time. During the conference a pastor came to us for counsel. He wanted to know what he had done wrong. There was a beautiful, young woman in her twenties who had been a Christian for only three months. She had come out of the occult and joined his church. The pastor described her as "on fire for the Lord." In fact, every week the church joined together at the altar to pray and fight the forces of darkness over their city. This woman was leading the assault.

However, one Wednesday evening something went wrong. As the zealous young woman stood up to rebuke and renounce Satan over her city, suddenly without warning, she dropped dead to the floor. The ambulance was called immediately, but it was too late. An autopsy was performed, but the doctors declared her death as a mystery.

The pastor cried as he finished his sad story. What did go wrong? We will never know. But there are at least four possibilities.

First, it's possible that this babe in Christ should not have been employed in this activity. In our military we don't send untrained recruits or the wounded to the front lines. In 1 John 2:13–14 John writes to three types of people: fathers, young men and dear children. He says, "I write to you, *fathers,* because you have known him who is from the beginning. I write to you, *young men,* because you have overcome the evil one. I write to you, *dear children,* because you have known the Father. I write to you, *fathers,* because you have known him who is from the beginning. I write to you, *young men,* because you are strong, and the word of God lives in you, and you have overcome the evil one" (emphasis added).

According to John's descriptions there are:

- Children who have known the Father

- Fathers who have known Him from the beginning

- Young men who are strong, who have the Word of God living in them and who have overcome the evil one

So as a new believer, the young woman may have had no spiritual authority to engage in this level of warfare because she lacked the required spiritual maturity. In too many cases, intercessors have almost lost their integrity with church leadership. We, the leaders of the prayer movement, must exercise wisdom in the following:

- What specific warfare assignments has Christ assigned to us?

- Whom has Christ called and prepared to engage in this warfare assignment?

- How will we prepare, and how long will it take to prepare for the assignment?

- When is the assignment to be carried out?

- What will be the real, measurable evidence that we have succeeded in the effort?

Until you have solid answers to these five questions, then it is not yet time for you to take action. God will hold leaders accountable for urging unqualified people into spiritual warfare. (See Hebrews 13:17.)

Second, sanctification and separation from sin often take time. Her spiritual authority may have been compromised by personal sin or occult alliances she had yet to renounce. Paul admonished each of us in Romans 12:1: "Therefore, I urge you, brothers, in view of God's mercy, to offer your bodies as living sacrifices, holy and pleasing to God—this is your spiritual act of worship." Before any of us enter into spiritual warfare, we should be living sacrifices, holy and pleasing to God.

Third, the young woman likely had very little biblical knowledge. In other words, she might have been fighting without the armor and, sadly, even a weapon. (See Ephesians 6:13–17.)

Finally, she might have slandered celestial beings without assignment. Jude 8–10 reminds us, "These dreamers pollute their own bodies, reject authority and slander celestial beings. But even the archangel Michael, when he was disputing with the devil about the body of Moses, did not dare to bring a slanderous accusation him, but said, 'The Lord rebuke you!'" As an untrained new believer, she may have been trying to prosecute Satan in heaven's court without the permission or directives of the lead attorney (Jesus). It is unfortunate but possible that she died as a result of her misled but determined actions to fight prematurely against the enemy. Only God knows for sure.

Because we have not allowed the Lord to deal with these issues of our own heart, Judge Jehovah *overrules* us due to tainted evidence.

"WE ARE THE CALLED"

One of our favorite TV commercials is the Marine Corps recruiting commercial. As the music swells, the swords between the Marine and unseen force are clashing, and the announcer boldly states, "We are the few...We are the proud...We are the Marines!"

Well, they may be the few and the proud, but *we are the called!* "And we know that all things work together for good to them that love God, to them who are the called according to his purpose" (Rom. 8:28, KJV). Like the Marines, we have an enemy to confront and a sword to wield. Ours is the sword of the Spirit (Eph. 6:17).

Jesus called us His friends: "I no longer call you servants, because a servant does not know his master's business. Instead,

I have called you friends, for everything that I learned from my Father I have made known to you. You did not choose me, but I chose you and appointed you to go and bear fruit—fruit that will last. Then the Father will give you whatever you ask in my name" (John 15:15–16). Even better news is that we "are being built into a spiritual house to be a holy priesthood" (1 Pet. 2:5). "You are a chosen people, a royal priesthood, a holy nation, a people belonging to God" (v. 9). With our credentials as kings and priests of God, Jesus' friends, the called of God, complete in Christ, forgiven and righteous, we are equipped with the Spirit's sword and qualified to prosecute the powers of darkness. But these qualifications have come as a result of Jesus Christ's fulfilling the Law on our behalf. Jesus said, "Do not think that I have come to abolish the Law or the Prophets; I have not come to abolish them but to fulfill them" (Matt. 5:17).

THE GROUNDWORK LAID

Before we could be released from death's grip and made alive before God, our sin had to be blotted out. Paul explained how Jesus' death eradicated our sin record, which resulted in disarming the devil and his angels. "Having canceled the written code, with its regulations, that was against us and that stood opposed to us; he took it away, nailing it to the cross. And having disarmed the powers and authorities, he made a public spectacle of them, triumphing over them by the cross" (Col. 2:14–15).

It is easy to understand how the devil had gained ground against us—we had fallen under Satan's dominion. Satan was pleading the law against us in the court of heaven, and he and the law were winning. Satan, just like any prosecuting attorney, has been presenting his charges and evidence against us as the defendants. With his endless accusations of men, he justly appealed to the righteousness of God as revealed by the law. We found ourselves condemned and confined to death row, where we were awaiting our final execution!

However, Jesus Christ fulfilled the law's demands by living a perfect life and dying in accordance with the Father's plan. He has delivered us from Satan's power. When Jesus was executed in our place, He once and for all settled our sin account.

John wrote, "My dear children, I write this to you so that you will not sin. But if anybody does sin, we have one who speaks to the Father in our defense—Jesus Christ, the Righteous One" (1 John 2:1). When Jesus pleads our case in heaven, He neither pleads our innocence nor our guilt; He pleads His blood. It is on the basis of His paying our penalty that the Governor (Jehovah) can justly issue our pardon and demand our release. The demands of justice have been satisfied, and Satan can no longer approach the Father demanding payment. That would constitute double jeopardy—the demand for a second payment for the same crime—which is illegal! The enemy's weapons have been stripped from his hands. Jesus has disarmed the devil of the right to condemn us. Hallelujah!

Paul recognized that Jesus had removed the handwriting of ordinances against us and that Satan could no longer legally accuse us before God. No charge against us will be entertained in court. Scripture says, "What, then, shall we say in response to this? If God is for us, who can be against us?... Who will bring any charge against those whom God has chosen? It is God who justifies. Who is he that condemns? Christ Jesus, who died— more than that, who was raised to life—is at the right hand of God and is also interceding for us" (Rom. 8:31, 33–34).

Notice the questions Paul submits: Who can be against us? Who is he that condemns? The definitive answer from heaven is *no one!* Although the devil's aim is to condemn us, God has justified us. All of our accounts are "Paid in Full." When it comes to heaven's courtroom, Satan's accusations of us now fall on deaf ears. Since God refuses to hear them, why are you listening?

Regis Philbin, the host of the popular show *Who Wants to Be a Millionaire?*, always asks the nervous player, "Is this your final answer?" Well, God has answered from heaven, "THIS IS MY FINAL ANSWER!"

The devil may contend with you, claiming that God will no longer help you. He is a liar when he suggests your sins prevent you from the right to prosecute him. Your authority against the principalities, powers and rulers of darkness is established as you stand on the biblical ground of what God has done for you and are following God's direct orders.

So why doesn't God just "zap" the devil and be done with it all? God will not do this for the same reason that He did not destroy Lucifer when he led angels and men into rebellion against God. When the Lord throws the devil into the lake of fire, sadly, because of His justice, He must also throw in people who are still aligned with Satan in sin. As a good and just God would, He has announced the promise of redemption through Jesus, His Son. He is still executing His plan of mercy for humanity as well as the final fiery judgment of Satan.

TWO VITAL POINTS

When we talk of spiritual warfare, some jump to the conclusion that we talk of speaking to Satan. Yet we overlook two vital points.

- *Satan is not omnipresent.* He cannot be at all places at all times. When we conduct warfare against the enemy, there is a high probability that it will not be Satan himself, but perhaps a high-ranking demon. Satan is likely busy working on heads of state and other nations that do his bidding.

- *Satan wants to lure us into a power struggle with his minions.* Some of us have not learned yet that Satan is a scrapper, a fighter, but he's not a lover. He wants to lure us into a power struggle with his demons. After all, fighting is fun to them. He can distract us from God's true assignments and deplete our energies as we fruitlessly shadowbox our supposed opponent.

Immature intercessors often fall victim to their own good intentions and, sometimes, to their own pride. They march arrogantly into enemy territory according to their own agenda. Some prayer warriors don't have a clue concerning the enemy's strength or the extent of his entrenchment. Unfamiliar with the rules of warfare engagement, they only guess about the strategy that the lead attorney, Jesus Christ, has formed. They have not been ordered to strike enemy headquarters. With Rambo-like techniques, these "lone rangers" lose their health, their families and for some, even their lives. It's one thing to lose these things out of obedience to the Commanding General. It's another thing to lose them all for naught. Wicked spirits love power encounters, especially when our pride is involved. Don't fall for it!

When our children were small, we did not teach them, "If a bully picks on you, just haul off and hit him as hard as you can!" No, we didn't! We said, "If a bully picks on you, come get me!" Our best definition and safest method of spiritual warfare is to "tattle." Tell God on the devil and his crowd! Ask for the Judge's intervention on your behalf or on behalf of the person or cause for which you are pleading.

"What about resisting Satan?" you ask. James wrote, "Submit yourselves, then, to God. Resist the devil, and he will flee from you. Come near to God and he will come near to you" (James 4:7–8). Resisting Satan always follows submitting to God. And submitting to God means to submit to His warfare strategy. It means to submit to the lead attorney's agenda. We don't taunt, mock or threaten Satan in and of ourselves, on our own. He knows that we are no match for him. However, when we draw near to God, God draws near to us. And Satan is no match for God!

FILE CHARGES AGAINST SATAN

Not every petition includes warfare proclamations. Only when you feel the Holy Spirit's prompting are you to directly address the enemy.

Clearly outline where your adversary (Satan) has violated the law. You are about to enter into spiritual warfare prayer. Satan has ceased in his role as prosecutor. You are now the prosecutor, and he has become the defendant. You are to prosecute him for his crimes against God and humanity. Write out the charges you wish to file against him.

In spiritual warfare prayer we...

- Sometimes declare Satan's guilt and demand justice (restoration).

- Sometimes seek his restriction (binding).

- Sometimes proclaim our enemy's punishment (loose something he has stolen).

- Sometimes petition God for protection from Satan (a legal *restraining order*).

A restraining order is an order of the court that prevents one party from contacting or approaching another. Jesus prayed for the Judge to issue a restraining order against Satan on behalf of His disciples and us when He prayed, "My prayer is not that you take them out of the world but that you protect them from the evil one" (John 17:15). In His model prayer, which we call the Lord's Prayer, Jesus taught us to ask the Judge for a restraining order against Satan for ourselves. He said that we should pray, "And lead us not into temptation, but deliver us from the evil one" (Matt. 6:13).

OUR ROLES AS PROSECUTORS

We have two roles when we stand as a prosecutor against the defendant Satan.

Prayer

In prayer we tell God the crimes the devil has committed and the laws he has broken, and we present our proof (the evidence). We prepare and present our case to the Judge so He can act upon it.

As prosecutors, using Scripture (the law) is essential to our prayer strategy. Without the Word as its foundation, every prayer hangs by a thread. Even prayer can be a worthless religious exercise. The Word of God empowers our prayer. It is the warhead on the missiles of prayer. Scripture grants us access in heaven and is the language of the court. If we don't know how to approach the Lord with His Word, prayer will continue to be a hit-and-run experience. To correctly position ourselves to present our case to the Judge, we should collect the relevant information. A good *prayer* warrior is a good *Word* warrior. "This is the confidence we have in approaching God: that if we ask anything according to his will, he hears us" (1 John 5:14).

Begin organizing and writing out your scriptures, prayer points and determining, with the Holy Spirit's leadership, how you plan to appeal to the Judge. For example:

> Father Judge, in the name of Jesus Christ our lead attorney, the enemy is accusing our pastor and his wife. Slanderous words are being spoken, and gossip is spreading like wildfire. But we have not been left defenseless. Heavenly Judge, according to Your Word, "It is time for you to act, O Lord; your law is being

broken" (Ps. 119:126). The powers of darkness are confusing his family, his church members and neighbors. The evidence is that "the wicked man hunts down the weak, who are caught in the schemes he [the devil] devises. He boasts of the cravings of his heart; he blesses the greedy and reviles the Lord" (Ps. 10:2–3).

Judge, I appeal to You. "Contend, O LORD, with those who contend with [us]; fight against those who fight against [us]" (Ps. 35:1). Because You are just, true and faithful, this is what I am asking You to do to the enemy. "For the sins of their mouths, for the words of their lips, let them be caught in their pride. For the curses and lies they utter, consume them in wrath, consume them till they are no more. Then it will be known to the ends of the earth that God rules over Jacob" (Ps. 59:12–13). As heaven's prosecutor I am asking You to:

- Act now against the forces of darkness.

- Notice that the enemy has broken Your law.

- Hunt down the wicked who oppress the man of God.

- Give help to the pastor, who is weak and tired and needs Your help.

- Take note of the arrogance of the devil, and cause him to fall.

- Expose the darkness, lies and confusion.

- Come and fight the demonic powers behind this situation.

- Deal harshly with the evil rulers that are tormenting.

- Fulfill Your divine purpose through this situation,

giving our friend a peace that You are working on his behalf.

Always keep in mind that we are not praying *against* people. We are to pray *for* people. We are wrestling in prayer against "spiritual wickedness in high places" (Eph. 6:12, KJV).

Proclamation

The second role we have is when we directly address evil spirits. Not all soldiers have the same responsibilities. There are different assignments in the army of God. But every assignment is important. It is important that you discover your calling and assignment in prayer and do not emulate others. Emulation is a work of the flesh (Gal. 5:20, KJV).

There may be times when the Lord will direct you to address the enemy directly. We use the same principles, but we will not engage in this type of warfare apart from the direct permission of our lead attorney, Jesus Christ. Regardless of the style, two things are clear. This is a real war. And the stakes are high. We are fighting for the souls of men, women, boys and girls. This battle is fought without guns or bullets. We fight it from our knees in intercessory prayer.

The following story describes this well.

> When a famous general from another nation visited America in 1921, he said in one of his speeches, "We must fight on our knees as well as in the trenches. The men of the infantry might advance on their stomachs, the tank crews in the tanks, the air force in planes, the navy in boats, but the church must advance on her knees."[2]

As the church advances on her knees, humility coupled with strength in God will determine her success in the courtroom. Jonathan Edwards was quoted as saying, "The best protection one can have from the devil and his schemes is a humble heart."[3] It's true. Most of Satan's fiery darts will miss their mark if we stay on our knees.

It is while on our knees that we can engage in direct proclamation against the forces of darkness. Our proclamation may be as follows:

> Spirits of darkness, I have been authorized by Jesus Christ, my lead attorney, to come against you. The Word of God says, "The reason the Son of God appeared was to destroy the devil's work" (1 John 3:8). "You belong to your father, the devil, and you want to carry out your father's desire. He was a murderer from the beginning, not holding to the truth, for there is no truth in him. When he lies, he speaks his native language, for he is a liar and the father of lies" (John 8:44). As a prosecutor on behalf of the court of heaven, I command you to loose my nephew (or whomever you name). In Jesus' name you are defeated, overcome by the blood of the Lamb. I break all contracts, covenants, alliances, iniquity of the forefathers, generational curses and unholy soul ties between you and my nephew. I remind you that Jesus said to me, "I have given you authority to trample on snakes and scorpions and to overcome all the power of the enemy; nothing will harm you" (Luke 10:19). By the evidence presented in court, I expose your deception, lies, fear and bondage. I send you out now in Jesus' name.

For a complete listing of the prayers David prayed against his enemies and to help you build your spiritual warfare vocabulary, read Eddie Smith's booklet, *Ammo! Building a Warfare Vocabulary.*

Finally, we continue to plead our cases against darkness as long as Jesus, our lead attorney, directs us. And we look for signs of the Judge's decision in each matter. There will always be physical manifestations of God's answer. We suggest that you begin to keep a scrapbook with newspaper clippings and other evidences that God has heard and answered your courtroom pleadings! Record your breakthroughs so you and others are encouraged and challenged.

The spectacle of a nation praying is more
awe-inspiring than the explosion of an atomic bomb.
The force of prayer is greater than any possible combination
of man-controlled powers because prayer is man's greatest
means of tapping the infinite resources of God.
—J. Edgar Hoover

Chapter 11

Purpose-Driven Prayer vs. Problem-Centered Praying

*I am convinced that the most outstanding enemy
in prayer is the lack of knowledge of what we are in Christ,
and what He is in us, and what He did for us, and of our
standing and legal rights before the throne.*
—E. W. KENYON

MANY years ago, a man with a hammer and chisel was working on the site of a new building. "Just what are you making out of that stone?" the visitor asked him.

"I don't know," the workman replied. "I haven't seen the plans; I am just chiseling."

There are millions of people who are "just chiseling" their way through life. They haven't seen the plans, but they feel compelled to keep busy, so they are chiseling. The same could be said for many intercessors (praying Christians). They keep chiseling away, praying and hoping that something, somewhere will change.

More important than prayer, as the title of George Otis's book indicates, is *Informed Intercession.* Informed intercession is praying in concert with the plans and purposes of God. Have you seen the plans? Or have you just been "chiseling?"

In Psalm 103:7 we read, "He made known his ways to Moses, his deeds to the people of Israel." The Israelites learned God's deeds—*what God did.* But they never learned *God's ways.* The deeds of God reveal *what* God does, but the ways of God reveal *how* and *why* He does it. This explains the difference between the way the children of Israel prayed and the way Moses prayed. To Moses, his relationship with God was to be cherished and nurtured. To the Israelites, God was little more than a "problem solver." They seemed never to see beyond their problem. They knew *about* God, but Moses *knew* God! Moses "chiseled" as one who had seen the plans! Seeing the plans—knowing God's purposes—will make a huge difference in our effectiveness as people of prayer.

GOD'S DEEDS—WHAT GOD DOES

Understanding *what* God does is the basis for the simplest prayer many of us learned to pray as small children. We heard our parents or other adults pray at meals, at church or at bedtime. We too began to ask God for things. The first bedtime prayer some of us learned was, "Now I lay me down to sleep. I pray the Lord my soul to keep. If I should die before I wake, I pray the Lord my soul to take." Your first mealtime prayer may have been, "God is great, God is good. Let us thank Him for our food."

Some of us learned to pray in school, especially before our final exams. We *really* learned to pray when things went wrong, because most of our praying was problem-centered. It had to do with finding solutions to our felt needs—and little more. We call this type of prayer "just chiseling." It is the most elementary form of prayer. Unfortunately, many of us never grow beyond this point. We must learn not only the *what* of prayer, but we are going to have to learn the *hows* and *whys* of prayer if we are going to become effective intercessory-attorneys. We must study the plans.

GOD'S WAYS—HOW GOD DOES WHAT HE DOES

First, it is important that we know how God solves our problems. Here is a brief list of how God solved problems in Scripture.

- *He caused a ram to be caught in a thicket.* Abraham was at the point of sacrificing his own son Isaac, when he saw "a substitute" (Gen. 22:1–18).

- *He split the Red Sea.* Moses, with one million upset Israelites, was trapped on the banks of the Red Sea, and an entire Egyptian army was pursuing them (Exod. 14).

- *He sent a living submarine, a whale, for Jonah.* Jonah had resisted the call to evangelize Nineveh, when a large fish takes him for a ride! (Jon. 1:12–2:10).

- *He caused an earthquake to effect a jailbreak.* Reread the story of Paul and Silas in prison in Acts 16, and you will notice that they weren't complaining that they had been beaten, nor were they looking for a way to escape. They weren't looking for a solution to their immediate problem. They knew the ways of God (God's plan) and were focused on the God of their problem!

- *He sent pizza by delivery ravens.* Elijah had just declared a drought to the wicked King Ahab, and Ahab was mad. God told Elijah to go hide (1 Kings 17:1–7).

- *He dropped down manna from heaven.* Moses' bunch was tired, hungry and grumbling when God ordered a special delivery meal for them (Exod. 16:1–22).

- *He prescribed seven dips in a dirty river.* Naaman, a sophisticated military captain, had leprosy. His instruction from the prophet seemed ridiculous (2 Kings 5:1–14).

- *He used everyday things—"spit" and "mud."* A man had been blind from birth. He wanted to be healed. No doubt this is the source of the popular toast "here's mud in your eye," which is another way of saying "here's to your health" (John 9:1–38).

Interesting solutions to people's problems, aren't they? Common to all of them is that they are creative, unique solutions. It is not surprising, then, that the first five words in Genesis present God as Creator. Genesis 1:1 says, "In the beginning God created..." The Hebrew word for *created* is *bara*. It means "to create something out of nothing." Judge Jehovah isn't into duplication. He is a creator. Creativity is central to how God sees and solves our problems.

Purpose-Driven Prayer vs. Problem-Centered Praying

When there are tasks to be done and problems to be solved, creators, like writers, designers and artists—the dreamers and visionaries—conceptualize the unseen solutions. They usually work instinctively, don't particularly like structure and are often frustrated by directions. Creators become pregnant with an idea until the concept becomes a reality. During this process, they impart a bit of themselves in the product. Well, our God is the consummate Creator.

People who only know *what* God does (His deeds) will tend to pray to God's productive side, rather than appeal to God's creative side. They pray with "problem-solving" in mind, often overlooking God's larger purpose. Rather than make their plea and submit the solution to Creator God and His plans, they want to instruct Him in their praying. Such requests frustrate a creator!

For us to be effective advocates, those who win decisions in heaven's court of law, we must learn not only *what* God does, but also *how* He does it. And *how* does God do what He does? Most of God's intervention in history has been as a creator.

So, when we pray, we should resist the urge to explain things to our omniscient God who knows all things. Let's also fight the urge to give Him directions on exactly how we want Him to solve our problem. Learn to see the big picture!

WHY GOD DOES WHAT HE DOES—HIS PURPOSES

How does God work? He works creatively. *Why* does He work? He works according to His purposes. God's decisions are always creative and always based on His purposes.

My dad (Alice) would close every prayer with the words, "In Jesus' name and for His sake, I pray, amen." We don't hear "and for His sake" much anymore. What does this actually mean? It means that I am submitting my request to God's purposes. For God has said, "For my own sake, for my own sake, I do this" (Isa. 48:11).

Why is always the more important question to ask. My (Eddie) father taught me, "The man who knows *how* will always work for the man who knows *why*." The Israelites knew *what* God did, but they did not know *why* He did it.

To effectively plead our cases in prayer in heaven's court, God's purposes—not just our problems—should be central to our praying. Although our problems are forever changing, God's purposes remain the same. He will ultimately act according to His purposes. We must learn His purposes to reach the highest level of prayer.

- "But the plans of the LORD stand firm forever, the purposes of his heart through all generations" (Ps. 33:11).

- "O great and powerful God, whose name is the LORD Almighty, great are your purposes and mighty are your deeds" (Jer. 32:18–19).

- "And we know that in all things God works for the good of those who love him, who have been called according to his purpose" (Rom. 8:28).

- "For it is God who works in you to will and to act according to his good purpose" (Phil. 2:13).

God's answer to your problem today will be creative, and it will be couched in His eternal purposes. The purposes of God are like gold to be mined from the promises of God.

There are two overriding purposes of God:

- The glory of His name—Exodus 3:15; 9:16; Malachi 1:11

- The establishment of His kingdom—Psalm 145:14; Habakkuk 2:14; Matthew 6:10

GOD'S PURPOSE REVEALED

Rest assured that anything God does for you in answer to your prayer will be done in accordance with these two primary goals. Nowhere is this principle seen more clearly than in Exodus 14.

The children of Israel had begun their exodus after four hundred years of servitude to the Egyptians. Pharaoh and his troops are hot on their heels when God tells the Israelites to camp near the sea.

> Then the LORD said to Moses, "Tell the Israelites to turn back and encamp near Pi Hahiroth, between Migdol and the sea. They are to encamp by the sea, directly opposite Baal Zephon."
>
> — EXODUS 14:1–2

Surely they asked why. Why were they to turn back and camp by the sea? To camp by the sea means you're trapped!

God responded to their questions by saying:

> Pharaoh will think, "The Israelites are wandering around the land in confusion, hemmed in by the desert." And I will harden Pharaoh's heart, and he will pursue them.
>
> —EXODUS 14:3–4

That couldn't have been encouraging news to Moses. After all, he was *himself* an Israelite! And God's instructions were:

- Camp in the open where Pharaoh's army can find you (v. 2).
- I will harden Pharaoh's heart (v. 4).
- He will pursue you (v. 4).

Imagine yourself under those circumstances. How would you have felt if you heard God say that to you? Some of us would have thought that the devil–not God–was talking to us.

Others would have begun seriously praying one of the following prayers:

- "God, please soften Pharaoh's heart," or
- "Send one more plague. Not flies, not frogs—this time we need a *major* plague, God!"

It is so easy for us to pray "out of our past" instead of praying according to God's purposes. It is easy to expect God to repeat Himself by what He does. Often when we feel trapped we will offer Him instructions.

But Moses and God shared an intimacy in prayer that the other Israelites didn't share. Moses, who wrote the Book of Exodus, reveals to us how he and God operated in prayer. Moses actually saw beyond his problems. He looked beyond God's deeds and saw God's ways, His purposes. God actually revealed His *purpose* to Moses in this situation! Moses was praying from a *kingdom perspective*, not a *problem perspective*.

And what was God's purpose?

> But I will gain glory for myself through Pharaoh and all his army, and the Egyptians will know that I am the LORD.
>
> —EXODUS 14:4

The children of Israel were hemmed in and about to be annihilated. What was on God's mind? Was it their plight, their problem? Sure. God knew their predicament. But never far from His thoughts is His own glory! He was going to answer them according to His purpose.

He said, "I will gain glory for myself through Pharaoh and all his army." Remember, Pharaoh had earlier determined that he was not going to glorify God. In Exodus 5:2 we hear Pharoah say, "Who is the LORD, that I should obey him and let Israel go? I do not know the LORD and I will not let Israel go." Exodus 8:15 says, "But when Pharaoh saw that there was relief, he hardened his heart and would not listen to Moses and Aaron, just as the Lord had said." There had been a time when Pharaoh had hardened his own heart; now God was hardening Pharaoh's heart. Never forget: God gets what He wants!

> So the Israelites did this. When the king of Egypt was told that the people had fled, Pharaoh and his officials changed their minds about them and said, "What have we done? We have let the Israelites go and have lost their services!" So he had his chariot made ready and took his army with him. He took six hundred of the best chariots, along with all the other chariots of Egypt, with officers over all of them. The Lord hardened the heart of Pharaoh king of Egypt, so that he pursued the Israelites, who were marching out boldly. The Egyptians—all Pharaoh's horses and chariots, horsemen and troops—pursued the Israelites and overtook them as they camped by the sea near Pi Hahiroth, opposite Baal Zephon.
>
> As Pharaoh approached, the Israelites looked up, and there were the Egyptians, marching after them. They were terrified and cried out to the Lord. They said to Moses, "Was it because there were no graves in Egypt that you brought us to the desert to die? What have you done to us by bringing us out of Egypt? Didn't we say to you in Egypt, 'Leave us alone; let us serve the Egyptians'? It would have been better for us to serve the Egyptians than to die in the desert!"
>
> —Exodus 14:4–12

The Israelites had only considered their immediate and rather serious problem. Not once had they considered God's purpose. For us to move from *problem-centered praying* to *purpose-driven praying* will require faith to look beyond our problems and see God's purposes. Faith removes mountains (Matt. 17:20). Faith sees beyond the horizon. We will have to do more than *chisel.* We are going to have to see the plans!

> Now faith is being sure of what we hope for and certain of what we do not see... By faith Noah, when warned about things not yet seen, in holy fear built an ark to save his family.
>
> —Hebrews 11:1, 7

Paul wrote, "So we fix our eyes not on what is seen, but on what is unseen. For what is seen is temporary, but what is unseen is eternal" (2 Cor. 4:18). When we embrace God's plan with our spiritual eyes of faith, we will be more committed to God's glory than to our success.

Look at Moses' statement of faith.

> Moses answered the people, "Do not be afraid. Stand firm and you will see the deliverance the Lord will bring you today. The Egyptians you see today you will never see again. The Lord will fight for you; you need only to be still."
>
> —Exodus 14:13–14

Moses saw something unseen. He gave the children of Israel six commands:

- Don't be afraid (v.13).
- Stand firm (v. 13).
- See the Lord's deliverance today (v. 13).
- See your enemy disappear (v. 13).
- The Lord will fight for you (v. 14).
- Be still (v. 14).

Then God responded to Moses' obedient leadership by instructing him, "Raise your staff and stretch out your hand over the sea to divide the water so that the Israelites can go through the sea on dry ground" (v. 16).

Now that's a novel solution! No one ever did *that* before! God continued His instruction to Moses:

> I will harden the hearts of the Egyptians so that they will go in after them. And I will gain glory through Pharaoh and all his army, through his chariots and his horsemen. The Egyptians will know that I am the LORD when I gain glory through Pharaoh, his chariots and his horsemen.
> —EXODUS 14:17–18

Here again we can see God's *purpose* in the solution! Three times in this chapter God says, "I will gain glory."

> Then the angel of God, who had been traveling in front of Israel's army, withdrew and went behind them. The pillar of cloud also moved from in front and stood behind them, coming between the armies of Egypt and Israel. Throughout the night the cloud brought darkness to the one side and light to the other side; so neither went near the other all night long.
> —EXODUS 14:19–20

Once again we see the creative solution of a creative God! God sent a pillar of cloud, with darkness on one side where the Egyptians were, and light on the other where God was leading the Israelites. We too will experience these kinds of glory if we will wait on His lead.

Moses became an active participant in God's creative solution for the children of Israel:

> Then Moses stretched out his hand over the sea, and all that night the LORD drove the sea back with a strong east wind and turned it into dry land. The waters were divided, and the Israelites went through the sea on dry ground, with a wall of water on their right and on their left.

> The Egyptians pursued them, and all Pharaoh's horses and chariots and horsemen followed them into the sea. During the last watch of the night the LORD looked down from the pillar of fire and cloud at the Egyptian army and threw it into confusion.
>
> —EXODUS 14:21–24

Another clever solution! The Egyptians were thrown into confusion as they followed into a sea of death. We read that God "made the wheels of their chariots come off so that they had difficulty driving" (v. 25).

Difficulty driving? No kidding! It's hard enough to drive a *wheeled* chariot in the sand, much less an *unwheeled* chariot! A chariot without wheels is a sled!

> And the Egyptians said, "Let's get away from the Israelites! The LORD is fighting for them against Egypt."
>
> —EXODUS 14:25

Good move on their part. Pharaoh was finally seeing the light. But as we say in Texas, "He's a day late and a dollar short!"

> Then the LORD said to Moses, "Stretch out your hand over the sea so that the waters may flow back over the Egyptians and their chariots and horsemen." Moses stretched out his hand over the sea, and at daybreak the sea went back to its place. The Egyptians were fleeing toward it, and the LORD swept them into the sea. The water flowed back and covered the chariots and horsemen—the entire army of Pharaoh that had followed the Israelites into the sea. Not one of them survived.
>
> —EXODUS 14:26–28

That was certainly a "red flag day" at the beach! That was a record-breaking undertow! Just as God had promised in verse

13, the enemy completely disappeared that day and was swept to the bottom of the sea!

> But the Israelites went through the sea on dry ground, with a wall of water on their right and on their left. That day the LORD saved Israel from the hands of the Egyptians, and Israel saw the Egyptians lying dead on the shore. And when the Israelites saw the great power the LORD displayed against the Egyptians, the people feared the LORD and put their trust in him and in Moses his servant.
>
> —EXODUS 14:29–31

The Israelites were no longer focusing on their problem, or even their solution. They were focusing on their God! As a result of their focus on their great God, they sing the first new song recorded in God's Word. You can read it in Exodus 15.

Everything that exists, including you and what you own, exists for God's purpose. "Thou art worthy, O Lord, to receive glory and honour and power: for thou hast created all things, and for thy pleasure [purpose] they are and were created" (Rev. 4:11, KJV).

Yes, even when solving our problems, the Father always acts according to His eternal purpose. Thousands of years later, Paul would remind us, "For the Scripture says to Pharaoh: 'I raised you up for this very purpose, that I might display my power in you and that my name might be proclaimed in all the earth'" (Rom. 9:17). Still today Jews tell the story of Pharaoh's defeat.

Even in spiritual warfare, God has His purposes. "To the intent that now unto the principalities and powers in heavenly places might be known by the church the manifold wisdom of God, according to the eternal purpose which he purposed in Christ Jesus our Lord" (Eph. 3:10–11, KJV). Simply put…God just loves to show off!

How does this relate to our pleading cases in prayer in

heaven's court? When we appeal in prayer to our Creator, we should expect that:

- He will express His creativity in the answer.
- He is about to do a new thing!
- He will express His ultimate purpose in the answer.
- Although His answers are forever changing, His eternal purposes do not change.

In John 9 we read of a man who was born blind. No doubt he had prayed many times for his healing. But when Jesus' disciples asked whose sins were responsible for his blindness, or why he was born blind, Jesus answered, "Neither this man nor his parents sinned . . . but this happened so that the work of God might be displayed in his life" (John 9:3). God had a purpose for allowing that man to be blind in his mother's womb. To pray effectively for such a man would have required taking God's purpose to heart.

As we mentioned briefly in an earlier chapter, in 2 Corinthians 12 we discover that the apostle Paul had a problem. He called it a "thorn in his flesh" (v. 7). Three times Paul asked God to remove this "messenger of Satan." But God's answer was *no.* Why did God say no? Why would God heal the blind man and not heal Paul? Strange to our limited reasoning, but it was for the same reason—for God's glory!

In Paul's case he knew why God didn't heal him. He knew God's purpose had to do with a revelation God had given him, a revelation so supreme that it provoked pride in Paul's heart. Jesus had said, "He that speaketh of himself seeketh his own glory" (John 7:18, KJV). Isaiah had written, "I am the LORD; that is my name! I will not give my glory to another" (Isa. 42:8). God told Moses, "But as truly as I live, all the earth shall be filled with the glory of the LORD" (Num. 14:21, KJV). If the whole earth is full of the glory of God, there is no place left for "the glory of

Paul," or for yours or ours for that matter.

So Paul explained, "To keep me from becoming conceited because of these surpassingly great revelations, there was given me a thorn in my flesh, a messenger of Satan, to torment me" (2 Cor. 12:7). We will never fully understand this, but God wouldn't have received as much glory in healing Paul as He did by presenting him to us as a "wounded warrior," totally dependent upon God, yet with sufficient grace to glorify Christ in the midst of hardship! So Paul said, "Therefore I will boast all the more gladly about my weaknesses, so that Christ's power may rest on me" (v. 9). A man who arrives at a place where he can boast in his infirmity is a man committed to the purposes of God.

The Father is concerned about us. He is interested in both healing our bodies and solving our problems, but not at the expense of His purposes. God is even more interested in demonstrating His power, glorifying His name and extending His kingdom in the earth.

DOING WHAT THE FATHER IS DOING

Problem-based praying identifies problems and forms appropriate requests. *Purpose-based praying* forms requests appropriate to God's purposes.

Jesus said, "I tell you the truth, the Son can do nothing by himself; he can do only what he sees his Father doing, because whatever the Father does the Son also does" (John 5:19). We should spend more time identifying and blessing what God *is* doing.

Consider your prayer life. When you pray for someone or something, do you begin with what you see God doing or with what you wish He were doing? We suggest that you:

- *Identify what God is doing.* What evidence, even subtle changes, do you see?

- *Thank God and praise Him for what He's doing.* Thank Him for the circumstances He is arranging, the people and the influences He is using and the miracles He is performing in this situation.

- *Proclaim His works.* Glorify His name.

- *Ask Him to enlarge the area of His activity.* Ask Him to demonstrate His power and glorify His name as He extends His kingdom in this matter.

Take city reaching for example. If you see a church in your city that is experiencing revival, what do you do? Is your primary prayer for God to touch the other churches? Or do you do what you see the Father doing? Do you partner with God in what He's doing by praying for the church He *is touching?* What would you pray?

- Thank Him for what He is doing.
- Ask Him to increase the move of the Spirit.
- Pray that He will expand this renewal to include every church in town.

Rather than continually asking God to do what He *is not doing,* bless what He *is doing!*

What is your problem today? Has it occurred to you to discover His purposes in your problem and to begin praying according to His purposes? Don't just "chisel." Take a look at the plans. God wants to do more than simply provide your solution. He wants to perform a demonstration of His miraculous, creative power, which will result in His name being glorified and His kingdom extended! Let's ask God to fulfill His purposes in solving our problems, which will result in His glory!

Our most successful intercession begins when, as the result of an intimate relationship with Him, we know the ways of God and pray accordingly. As we pray, let's expect that His solution will be creative! Don't instruct the Creator! Expect something new. Don't lecture God. Remind Him of His Word, ask Him for a breakthrough and prepare yourself for the unexpected!

> Live for something, have a purpose,
> And that purpose keep in view;
> Drifting like a helpless vessel
> You can never to life be true.
>
> Half the wrecks that strew life's ocean,
> If some star had been their guide,
> Might have now been safely riding,
> But they drifted with the tide.
>
> —Author unknown[1]

Rejoice, friend! The dilemma you have today is an opportunity for a demonstration of God's miraculous, creative power to be displayed! (See James 1:2.)

FINAL WORD

Charles Plumb, a Naval Academy graduate and fighter pilot in Vietnam, flew seventy-five combat missions and then had his plane destroyed by a surface-to-air missile. He ejected from his plane and parachuted into enemy hands, was captured and spent six years in a Communist prison. Charles survived the ordeal and now delivers lectures about the lessons learned from that experience.

One day when Plumb and his wife were sitting in a restaurant, a man at another table came up and said, "You're Plumb! You flew fighters in Vietnam from the *Kitty Hawk*, and you were shot down!"

"How in the world did you know that?" asked Plumb.

"I packed your parachute," the man replied. Plumb gasped in

surprise and graciously expressed his gratitude to the man.

The man leaned forward and shook his hand, saying, "I guess it worked!"

Plumb assured him, "It sure did. If the chute you prepared hadn't worked for me, I wouldn't be here today!"

Charles Plumb couldn't sleep that night, thinking about the man. Plumb continues, "I kept wondering what the sailor might have looked like in a Navy uniform—a Dixie-cup hat, a bib in the back and bell-bottom trousers. I wondered how many times I might have seen him and not even said, 'Good morning. How are you?' Because you see, I was a fighter pilot, and he was just a sailor."

Plumb thought of the many hours the sailor had spent at a long wooden table, in the bowels of the ship carefully weaving the shrouds and folding the silks of each parachute, each time holding in his hands the fate of someone who didn't even know who he was.

Now when Plumb speaks, he asks his audience, "Who's packing your parachute?"[2]

We would like to pose a different question. Our question is, *Whose parachute are you packing?* Are you willing to be an advocate for others? Whose life is hanging in the balance, where your intercession is the determining factor? Heaven is waiting to hear your answer. Will the Honorable Judge Jehovah hear you say, "Yes, I *will* be an advocate?"

> *Be self-controlled and alert. Your enemy the devil prowls around like a roaring lion looking for someone to devour. Resist him, standing firm in the faith, because you know that your brothers throughout the world are undergoing the same kind of sufferings.*
> —1 Peter 5:8–9

Appendix A
Glossary of Terms

Accusation–A charge or an allegation of fact

Adversary–An opponent or enemy

Advocate–One who speaks on behalf of another

Appeal–A proceeding by which one seeks a court review of a former court's decision

Argue–To contend or reason together

Attorney–A lawyer or legal representative in court

Attorney of record–The lead attorney who directs the case

Case–A project that a lawyer works on for a client

Chambers–A place, usually a private room or office of the judge in the courthouse, where a judge hears motions, signs papers or conducts other business when not presiding over a session of court

Client–A customer, a person facing trial

Compensatory damages–Monetary reimbursement for actual loss or injury

Counselor–Another word for attorney, lawyer or advocate

Court–The place for legal confrontation

Court-appointed attorney–A defense attorney the court assigns to a case

Cross-examination–The questioning of a defendant by the opposing attorney

Death penalty–A judge's decree to terminate the life of the accused

Decision–The judgment or decree of a court upon a matter before it

Defendant–The party against whom an action is brought and who defends or answers the legal action

Defense–To plead the case for another

Defense attorney–An attorney who pleads the case of another

Double Jeopardy–The constitutional prohibition against a second prosecution of a person for the same crime

Evidence–Information that helps a lawyer prove a point

Incompetent Evidence–Evidence that is not admissible under the rules of evidence

Injustice–A miscarriage of the law

Intercessor–One who stands in the gap for another (as their advocate) in prayer

Judge–A public official who administers the law by presiding over courts, arbitrating disputes and advising lawyers, juries, parties engaged in lawsuits and court personnel

Judgment–The official decision of a court determining the rights of the parties involved, the pronouncement of guilt and/or the sentence, unless the defendant has been acquitted

Jurisdiction–The sphere of one's authority under the law

Jurisprudence–In the United States, both "law" in a general sense and the study of law

Jury–Literally, a panel of judges

Lawyer–A trained professional who represents a client in working out laws that govern society

Lead Attorney–The attorney of record who directs the case

Perjury–Giving false testimony under oath in court

Petitioner–One on whose behalf a petition is presented to a court or other official body

Plaintiff–A person who initiates an action, suit or complaint in court against another

Plea–An allegation or defense of a party in a legal proceeding (such as a plea of "guilty" or "not guilty" in response to a criminal charge)

Plead a case–To argue a case in court

Pleadings–Formal written allegations by the parties containing their respective claims and defenses

Precedent–A decision of the court from the past that guides the judges and juries in the same or similar issues

Prosecutor–A trial attorney representing the State in criminal cases

Punitive (or exemplary) damages–Money awarded in addition to compensatory damages, as a penalty for a wrong committed

Restraining Order–A court's order to prevent one party from contacting or approaching another

Satan–The devil, our adversary in court

Sentence–To pass judgment or condemn

Solicitor–A designation for the prosecuting official representing the State in certain jurisdictions

Trial–The proceedings within the courtroom

Verdict–The official decision of a jury as reported to and accepted by the court

Appendix B
Examples of Scripture Prayers

A FATHER'S PRAYER—FROM EDDIE'S PRAYER DIARY

Lord God of heaven and earth, I place my child (name) in Your hands, and I ask You to establish what You have written in Proverbs 4 in his life today.

Today I come before You to petition the court of heaven. Father God, cause my child to listen to Your instruction and to mine. (See verse 1.)

May the things that You, his mother and I have taught reverberate in his heart and mind day and night. (See verses 4, 20–21.) May those truths awaken him in the night and interrupt him in the day. May Your truth convict, draw, humble and move him in Your direction, O God.

I don't ask this for my child's sake, his mother's sake or for my sake. I ask it for Your sake and for Your kingdom's sake.

I bring before You, Judge of heaven, the promises that You have made to his mother and me. I bring before Your court the promises in Your Word concerning me and my children.

I bring before You the visions and dreams You have given us concerning him.

On the basis of this irrefutable evidence, evidence collected from this very court, I ask for a swift rendering of judgment on this matter, O God. I ask that Your gavel fall. Speak the Word, and my son will return to You, to his mother and me in humility and holiness. Establish Your righteous kingdom in his heart. Lead him to life everlasting, and cause him to walk in Your ways!

A PRAYER FOR OUR CHILDREN— FROM PSALM 103 AND 1 JOHN 1

Judge of heaven, You have stated that Your righteousness extends unto the children's children.

I stand before Your throne today, great Judge of the universe, and implore You to detonate an explosion of righteousness in the hearts of my children (name them). As an attorney for their defense, I pray that Your righteousness will overtake their thinking, invade their sleeping and sweep over and through their being with such a force that it will impact their world!

Lord, I remind You of Psalm 103:18, and that their mother and I have sought to keep Your covenant and remember Your commands to do them. Admittedly, we have not done so perfectly, Your honor. Therefore, I call into evidence court's Exhibit B—the blood of Your own Son, Jesus. (See 1 John 1:9.)

Your Honor, both You and He have established that His blood justifies their mother and me. Therefore I ask that it be applied to our account that this promise of Yours might be immediately enforced.

As a prosecuting attorney, I ask that You place a heavenly restraining order around my children, their mother and me so that the evil one will be kept at a distance. Arrest him should he or his assigns be found in violation of the court's order.

Finally, Your Honor, as Your angels who excel in strength keep Your commandments and hear the voice of Your Word bless You...so do I.

As Your hosts and ministers that do Your pleasure bless you...so do I.

As Your works in all places of Your dominion bless you...my soul blesses You!

Be blessed, Lord of heaven. (See Psalm 103:20–22.)

A PRAYER FROM PSALM 103:17–19

Father in heaven, I bless You today and exalt Your name. You alone are holy. You alone are worthy of praise. You alone are to be exalted. You alone are life. You are the I AM, You alone!

I bring these words before Your throne, great Judge, eternal Judge, awesome Judge of heaven. You have spoken. Your decree has gone forth. You have pronounced Your proclamation.

I do not come asking the court for mercy. You are merciful. I do not come asking the court for grace. You are gracious. I do not come asking the court to render an opinion on the matter. For this matter was settled for eons. I do not ask the court for a decision on this matter. You have decided!

I only ask today that You enforce Your decision in this matter. I ask that You activate Your conclusion and bring it to pass in my specific case.

Lord of the universe, You have said that Your mercy is from everlasting to everlasting upon him that fears You. Your Honor, today (this day) fits into this time frame.

You have written that Your throne is prepared "in the heavenlies" and that Your "kingdom rules over all." Sir, "all" includes the first realm in which my family and I live. It includes the realm in which our ministry operates. Further, Your Honor, "all" includes the second heaven in which the prince of darkness, his princes and their minions reside. Nothing, and no one, is out from under Your jurisdiction, for You rule over all!

Your Honor, You have declared that Your mercy is upon those who fear You. My wife and I fear you, O Lord. You are the only God and above all others and all things. Therefore, I call upon the mercy that rests upon me today. I humbly ask in faith that You respond to Your own words and activate Your mercy to me in the following ways ... (List your request.)

A PRAYER FROM PSALM 148:1—4, 7—12

Father, I bless You today for who You are. I praise You with the heavens, the heights, the angels, the heavenly host, the sun, the moon, the shining stars, the highest heavens, the waters above the skies, the great sea creatures, the ocean depths, lightening and hail, snow and clouds, stormy winds, mountains and hills, fruit trees and cedars, wild animals and cattle, small creatures, flying birds, kings of the earth, all nations, princes and rulers on earth, young men and maidens, old men and children.

A PRAYER FROM PSALM 146:6—10

Lord in heaven, I praise You for what You have done. You are my Maker. You uphold the oppressed. You feed the hungry. You set prisoners free. You give sight to the blind. You lift up the downhearted. You love the righteous. You watch over the stranger. You sustain the fatherless and the widow. You frustrate the ways of the wicked. You reign forever. You listen to me, and You hear my prayer!

Appendix B: Examples of Scripture Prayers

A PRAYER FROM PSALM 67

Heavenly Father, be gracious unto my family and me today. Bless us, I pray. Let Your face so shine upon us that Your ways may be known on earth and Your salvation be known by all people. May the nations of the earth be glad, sing for joy and praise You because You rule them all justly and guide them. Lord, You guide the nations, command the money and cause the land to yield its financial harvest. You are just and most worthy of praise. Bless us, I pray. Meet our financial needs according to Your mercy, Your abundant mercy, for Christ's glory!

A PERSONAL PRAYER

Father, bless me and show me Your grace. Make Your face shine upon me. Let me, my life and my family, as we relate to You, show the world Your ways and Your salvation. Then they will be glad and sing for joy and will praise You.

PRAYER FOR AN UPCOMING CONFERENCE

Father, I thank You for the privilege of partnership with You in producing this conference on prayer. You are the purpose, and Your desires and plans are primary. Since I don't know them, I pray that your Holy Spirit will guide every word and lead us in the steps we should take.

You have said, "No one knows the thoughts of God except the Spirit of God. We have ... received ... the Spirit who is from God, that we may understand" (1 Cor. 2:11–12). I have received the Spirit of God. Holy Spirit, cause me to understand the Father's purposes and desires for this conference. Not that I can cause them to come to pass, but so I can keep from being a hindrance to them. I thank You for understanding.

As You showed Moses how to build the tabernacle in Exodus 26, show me now how to facilitate this conference. As You told Elijah how to build the altar upon which fire fell in 1 Kings 18, show me how to work with You here, that Your fire might fall here as well.

Finally, Lord, once You've challenged Your people and changed them, I pray that You will provide for the financial challenge of this conference. As we give generous honorariums to the speakers, Your ministers, I pray that You will give to our ministry "good measure, pressed down, shaken together, and running over" (Luke 6:38).

I ask for all the costs to be covered. Thank You for Your faithfulness. You have done this for us in the past. You have done this for others. It is an example of Your gracious and generous heart, Lord of the universe.

Great Judge of heaven, I plead this case before You today asking that You honor Your Word and Your Son on our behalf. I ask that You demonstrate Your power in this regard.

Notes

Chapter 1
The Trials of Life

1. Paul E. Holdcraft, *Cyclopedia of Bible Illustrations* (New York/Nashville: Abingdon-Cokesbury Press, 1947), 9.
2. Ibid.
3. David Bryant, "Standing Up for Others," in Dr. Cornell Haan, *The Lighthouse Devotional* (Sisters, OR: Multnomah Publishers, 2000), 215.

Chapter 2
Job's School of Suffering

1. "I've Got Confidence" by Andraé Crouch, copyright © 1969 100% Bud John Songs, Inc./ASCAP. Admin. by EMI Christian Music Publishing. Used by permission. All rights reserved.
2. Craig Brian Larson, *Illustrations for Preaching and Teaching* (Grand Rapids, MI: Baker Books, 1993), 11.
3. Reported to us by May-on Tchao, who coordinated the Spiritual Warfare and Spiritual Mapping Conference we conducted in Hong Kong in June 1999.

Chapter 3
Mr. Christian Goes to Court

1. Paul Aurandt, *More of Paul Harvey's The Rest of the Story,* as told in Charles R. Swindoll, *The Tale of the Tardy Oxcart* (Nashville: Word, 1998), 496.
2. Bob Terrell and Marcellus "Buck" Buchanan, *Disorder in the Court* (Asheville, NC: Bright Mountain Books, Inc., 1984).
3. Milburn H. Miller, *Notes and Quotes for Church Speakers* (Anderson, IN: Warner Press, 1960), 103.

4.   Bruce Lockerbie, *Fatherlove,* as told in Swindoll, *The Tale of the Tardy Oxcart,* 204.

5.   Larson, *Illustrations for Preaching and Teaching,* 46.

6.   Bruce Larson, *Setting Men Free,* as told in Swindoll, *The Tale of the Tardy Oxcart,* 214.

7.   A. Bernard Webber, *Choice Illustrations and Quotable Poems* (Grand Rapids, MI: Zondervan Publishing House, 1944), 54.

CHAPTER 4
JESUS CHRIST, THE ATTORNEY OF RECORD

1.   Elisabeth Elliott, *A Slow and Certain Light,* as told in Larson, Illustrations for Preaching and Teaching, 106.

2.   *Encyclopedia Britannica,* vol. 18 (Chicago/London/Toronto: William Benton, publisher, 1960), 386–387.

3.   Haan, *The Lighthouse Devotional,* 289.

CHAPTER 5
SATAN, OUR ADVERSARY IN COURT

1.   Ewald M. Plass, *What Luther Says: An Anthology,* vol. 1, as told in Swindoll, *The Tale of the Tardy Oxcart,* 154.

2.   Oswald Chambers, *My Utmost for His Highest* (New York: Dodd, Mead and Company, 1935), 351.

3.   "The Pen Pal," author unknown. Source obtained from the Internet: www.dnc.net/users/garrenmg/hearts/penpal.htm.

CHAPTER 6
HERE COMES THE JUDGE!

1.   Dr. William Smith, *Smith's Bible Dictionary,* s.v. "jasper." Source obtained from the Internet: bible.crosswalk.com/Dictionaries/SmithsBibleDictionary/smt.cgi?number=T2274.

2.   Larson, *Illustrations for Preaching and Teaching,* 25.

3.   Miller, *Notes and Quotes for Church Speakers,* 102.

4.   From the hymn "Great Is Thy Faithfulness" by Thomas O. Chisholm, copyright © 1923, ren. 1951 Hope Publishing Company, Carol Stream, IL 60188. All rights reserved. Used by permission.

5.   Miller, *Notes and Quotes for Church Speakers,* 119.

Notes

Chapter 7
Personal Preparation

1. G. B. F. Hallock, *Best Modern Illustrations* (New York: Harper and Brothers Publishers, 1935), 283.
2. Alan D. Wright, *Lover of My Soul* (Sisters, OR: Multnomah Publishers, 1998), 179.
3. Source unknown.
4. Alice Smith, *Beyond the Veil* (Ventura, CA: Regal Publishing Co., 1997), 118.
5. "Leave It There" by Charles Albert Tindley. Public domain.
6. Holdcraft, *Cyclopedia of Bible Illustrations,* 262.
7. Hallock, *Best Modern Illustrations,* 116.
8. Bruce Larson, *Wind and Fire,* as told in Larson, *Illustrations for Preaching and Teaching,* 129.
9. Hallock, *Best Modern Illustrations,* 183.
10. Ibid., 274.

Chapter 8
Case Preparation: Defending Others in Court

1. Larson, *Illustrations for Preaching and Teaching,* 66.
2. C. H. Spurgeon, "Order and Argument in Prayer." Sermon delivered at Metropolitan Tabernacle, Newington, July 15, 1866.
3. *People* magazine (March 1999), 66.
4. Source unknown.

Chapter 9
Win or Lose?

1. Larson, *Illustrations for Preaching and Teaching,* 73.
2. Dick Eastman, *No Easy Road* (Grand Rapids, MI: Baker Book House, 1971), 97–98.
3. Larson, *Illustrations for Preaching and Teaching,* 183.
4. Haan, *The Lighthouse Devotional,* 47.

Chapter 10
Warfare Prayer: Prosecuting Satan in Court

1. Hallock, *Best Modern Illustrations,* 112.

2. Miller, *Notes and Quotes for Church Speakers,* 138.
3. Frank S. Mead, *12,000 Religious Quotations,* as used in Swindoll, *The Tale of the Tardy Oxcart,* 280.

CHAPTER 11
PURPOSE-DRIVEN PRAYER VS. PROBLEM-CENTERED PRAYING

1. Holdcraft, *Cyclopedia of Bible Illustrations,* 298.
2. Adapted from Greg Albrecht, *Plain Truth Magazine* (January/ February 2000), 25.

Subject Index

Index

Index

Index

medium: 159
mental aerobics: 98
mentor: 100
Messiah: 89, 92
methods: 5, 76, 159
MIA: 17, 18
Micaiah: 82
Mickey Bonner: 101
Migdol: 181
mighty God: 89
Milburn H. Miller: 201
military: 138, 161, 178
militia: 17
mill: 9
millions: 3, 42, 55, 112, 123, 176
missile: 169, 191
mission trip: 42
mocked: 32
model: 107, 114, 168
Moline, Illinois: 45
monitoring: 29, 104, 139
morality: 27
morals: 5
Moses: 11, 22, 44, 83–84, 101, 114,
    123–126, 141, 149, 163, 176–178,
    181–188, 200
motives: 117, 121, 140
motor home: 13–16
Mount Carmel: 141
Mount Washburn: 93
Mrs. Jenkins: 4–5
Multnomah Publishers: 201
mystical: 26

N

natural disasters: 5
Naval Academy: 191
navy: 171, 192
needy: 155
Nestor: 98
new belief system: 98
new birth: 6, 75–76, 98–99
New Testament: 29, 87, 123
New York City: 26, 77
New Yorker: 53

Nike: 42
No Easy Road: 203
Noah: 84, 90, 184
Notes and Quotes: 201, 202, 204
nuclear blast: 84
nurse: 86, 123

O

O. J. Simpson: 60
oath: 69, 194
objectivity: 105
occult: 161–162
offense: 94
Old Testament: 22, 44, 87, 126
oldest rule: 68
omnipotent: 85, 95
omnipresent: 22, 85, 166
omniscient: 47, 85, 90–91, 179
opponent: 122, 167, 193
oppressor: 129, 155, 158
Order and Argument in Prayer: 112,
    203
Oriental: 113
Oswald Chambers: 58, 76, 109, 157,
    202
outcome: 60, 62, 76, 129
outer shell: 9
overrules: 163
Oxford University: 151

P

Paid in Full: 165
pallet: 38
panda bears: 95
parachute: 191–192
parakletos: 44
paralegals: 60, 117
partnership: 73, 199
patient: 25, 48, 58, 89, 90–91
Patmos: 82
patrolman: 46, 93
Paul Daniel Rader: 105
peace of God: 89, 140
peace with God: 89
peaceful: 38, 88

Index

Index

THE MINISTRY OF CHRIST THROUGH
EDDIE & ALICE SMITH
U.S. PRAYER CENTER

- ### Conferences, Seminars, Retreats
  Eddie and Alice Smith travel worldwide teaching together and separately on various themes related to revival and spiritual awakening. Topics include prayer, intercession, deliverance, worship, spiritual warfare and spiritual mapping. If you would like additional information about hosting an event with Alice or Eddie in your church or city, contact our office at (713) 466-4009 or visit our website at www.usprayercenter.org.

- ### Books, Tapes and Other Resources
  The Smiths have produced many resources relating to subjects they teach. Books they have written include *Beyond the Veil: Entering Into Intimacy With God Through Prayer; Intercessors: How to Understand and Unleash Them for God's Glory; Intercessors & Pastors: The Emerging Partnership of Watchmen & Gatekeepers* and many other small booklets. You will find their books, tapes, seminars on tape, and more at www.prayerbookstore.com.

- ### *PrayerNet* Newsletter
  Alice Smith is editor of this up-to-the-minute, informational and inspirational, biweekly e-mail newsletter. It's FREE! Join thousands of others worldwide who receive *PrayerNet* by sending a "blank" email message to prayernet-subscribe@usprayercenter.org.

- ### *UpLink* Newsletter
  UpLink is a newsletter designed to inspire and inform about prayer mailed to subscribers (in the U.S.) monthly. To receive *UpLink,* call us tollfree at (800) 569-4825.

- ### *PrayUSA!*
  Since 1997, Eddie and Alice have coordinated 40 days of prayer and fasting for revival and spiritual awakening in the United States each spring during the Lenton season, Ash Wednesday through Palm Sunday. CBN News has described *PrayUSA!* as the largest prayer and fasting initiative in history. It now works with *PrayWORLD!* to mobilize millions around the world to synchronized prayer for their nations through the same 40-day calendar each year. Visit our website for more information about PrayUSA! at www.usprayercenter.org.

EDDIE & ALICE SMITH
U.S. PRAYER CENTER
7710-T Cherry Park Dr., PMB 224
Houston, TX 77095
Phone: (713) 466-4009
Fax: (713) 466-5633
www.usprayercenter.org